A Good Quarrel

AMERICA'S TOP LEGAL REPORTERS SHARE STORIES FROM INSIDE THE SUPREME COURT

A Good Quarrel

AMERICA'S TOP LEGAL REPORTERS SHARE STORIES FROM INSIDE THE SUPREME COURT

Timothy R. Johnson
and Jerry Goldman
EDITORS

With a Foreword by
RICHARD J. LAZARUS

FIRST INDIAN REPRINT, 2011

Universal
Law Publishing Co. Pvt. Ltd.
NEW DELHI - INDIA

First Indian Reprint, 2011

ISBN: 978-93-5035-036-2

Published by
UNIVERSAL LAW PUBLISHING CO. PVT. LTD.
C-FF-1A, Dilkhush Industrial Estate (Near Azadpur Metro Station)
G.T. Karnal Road, Delhi-110 033
Tel.: 011- 42381334, 27215334, 27438103, Fax : 011-27458529
E-mail *(For sales inquiries)* : sales@unilawbooks.com
Website : www.unilawbooks.com

Under Special arrangement with
THE UNIVERSITY OF MICHIGAN PRESS, USA.

A CIP catalog record for this book is available from the British Library.

Library of Congress Cataloging-in-Publication Data

A good quarrel : America's top legal reporters share stories from inside the Supreme Court / edited by Timothy R. Johnson and Jerry Goldman ; with a foreword by Richard J. Lazarus.

p. cm.

Includes index.

ISBN-13: 978-0-472-11636-2 (cloth : alk. paper)

ISBN-10: 0-472-11636-3 (cloth : alk. paper)

ISBN-13: 978-0-472-03326-3 (pbk. : alk. paper)

ISBN-10: 0-472-03326-3 (pbk. : alk. paper)

1. United States. Supreme Court—History—Sources. 2. Forensic orations—United States. 3. Constitutional history—United States—Sources. I. Johnson, Timothy R., 1971- II. Goldman, Jerry.

KF8742.G66 2009

347.73'26—dc22 2009007716

Printed in India at Glorious Printers, New Delhi

For my dad, who instilled in me a love of politics—TRJ

For J. Woodford Howard, Jr., mentor—JG

I saw no man use you a pleasure; if I had, my weapon should quickly have been out, I warrant you: I dare draw as soon as another man, if I see occasion in a good quarrel, and the law on my side.

—*Romeo and Juliet,* act II, scene 4

FOREWORD

An oral argument before the Supreme Court may well be the most fascinating, almost mystical, aspect of our nation's lawmaking process. Private citizens cannot join the president and the cabinet in the White House when they debate urgent policy matters. Private citizens cannot appear in the well of Congress, admonishing lawmakers to pass needed legislation. But ironically, the most private of our three branches of government offers the public moments with private attorneys representing clients taking center stage.

Perhaps that is why the opportunity to present oral argument before the Court is almost every lawyer's fantasy. To become part of and perhaps even to shape the nation's history through the power of persuasion. To join the ranks of some of the nation's most historic and colorful figures who have also stood at the lectern facing a barrage of questions from the chief justice and associate justices: Daniel Webster, who would literally start his arguments over again if some "ladies" entered late and missed his opening; eight different presidents of the United States, including John Quincy Adams, Abraham Lincoln, and Richard Nixon; and spectacular advocates who went on to join the Court itself, including the nation's most famous chief justice, John Marshall, who is credited with establishing the essential independence of the federal judiciary; Justice Thurgood Marshall, whose brilliant advocacy culminated in *Brown v. Board of Education;* and the current chief justice, John G. Roberts Jr., widely considered the best advocate of his generation, who argued thirty-nine cases before the Court, more than anyone else who went on to join the Court.

Oral argument before the Court is certainly not for the fainthearted. Several advocates have nevertheless done just that—fainted. Thomas Ewing, a senator from Ohio, fainted while presenting argument in 1869, and his son, General Thomas Ewing, did the same twenty-six years later on the same spot. Another counsel collapsed unconscious to the floor when Justice William O. Douglas demanded to know who had prepared a particular affidavit in the case; after recovering, the attorney stood up and gamely acknowledged that he had. Today's justices are no less demanding in the rigor, persistence, or number of questions. Today's Court is a hot—sometimes even scalding—bench. Chief Justice Roberts recently recalled being asked more than one hundred questions during one of his arguments.

Does oral argument matter? Absolutely. The old adage holds that cases can never be won at oral argument, only lost. The latter is true, but the former is not. Although written briefs constitute the most important aspect of advocacy, the oral argument is where the deal can be closed—or not. It is the first time that the justices talk about the case together; it is almost always the single largest amount of time that they will ever spend discussing the case; and it is when they first learn what the other justices are thinking. Lawyers have the enormous opportunity to participate in that conversation, to learn about individual justices' concerns, and to address those concerns. At oral argument, a justice's outlook often perceptibly shifts as concerns are addressed and misconceptions are erased. The Court's opinion can be influenced in significant ways, as can the Court's judgment.

This book brings to life with written words and accompanying audio recordings the magic of oral argument before the Supreme Court. The chapter authors include the nation's top journalists who cover the Court, a notoriously challenging beat. These reporters combine a sophisticated understanding of the Court with the ability to tell a great story. And the stories they have produced in this book are wonderful.

They are stirring, illuminating, and brutally honest. The stories provide a ready reminder that the justices are not there for show, have difficult issues to decide, and have high expectations of the advocates as "officers of the Court" to answer the questions justices pose.

For those who are prepared to provide such assistance, a Supreme Court argument can truly represent a professional pinnacle. Attorneys can indeed become part of the nation's history and even play a significant role in shaping that history. But for those who are not, appearing before the Court does not present a pretty picture.

Read, listen, and enjoy.

Richard J. Lazarus

CONTENTS

Preface | xiii

Introduction:
The Role of Oral Arguments in the Supreme Court
TIMOTHY R. JOHNSON AND JERRY GOLDMAN | 1

Elk Grove Unified School District v. Newdow:
Ten Commandments of Oral Arguments
DAHLIA LITHWICK | 11

Forsyth County, Georgia v. the Nationalist Movement:
A Workman-like Performance
TIM O'BRIEN | 20

Planned Parenthood of Southeastern Pennsylvania v. Casey:
The Rhetorical Battle over *Roe*
LYLE DENNISTON | 42

Bush v. Gore:
Preparing for Oral Combat—the Fight for the Presidency
CHARLES BIERBAUER | 61

Glickman v. Wileman Brothers and Elliott Inc.:
How Oral Arguments Led to a Lawsuit
TONY MAURO | 74

Grutter v. Bollinger:
An Argument for the Ages
GREG STOHR | 98

Chandler v. Miller:
Double Indemnity
NINA TOTENBERG | 110

Rapanos v. United States:
Wading into the Wetlands
DAVID G. SAVAGE | 125

Randall v. Sorrell:
Arguing over Campaign Finance in Vermont
BRENT KENDALL | 145

UAAAIWA v. Johnson Controls Inc.:
Fighting for Women's Rights in the Workplace
STEVE LASH | 158

Time Inc. v. Hill:
A Future President Makes His Case
FRED GRAHAM | 169

Acknowledgments | 179

Works Cited | 181

Contributors | 185

Index | 189

PREFACE

A Good Quarrel offers eleven firsthand accounts of arguments before the U.S. Supreme Court. While reading the following analyses of landmark Supreme Court cases, provided by some of the best court reporters in the nation, you—the reader—can listen to audio files of these same Supreme Court arguments in one of two ways. Beginning at the web site **www.goodquarrel.com,** you can click on each case and simply listen through your computer. But if you prefer to leave your computer behind and listen to the audio on-the-go or as you read the book, then you can download the MP3 files to an MP3 player.

Whichever method you choose, the audio supplements for each chapter are available on the **www.goodquarrel.com** web site in the following manner.

- The **Clips** link refers to the clips our authors have chosen to demonstrate particular points in their analysis. In the book you will know it is time to click on a clip when you see this symbol: 🔊. These clips appear in page order in the book, and we reference each one with a page number as well as with a short description.
- You can also click on **Oral Argument,** which allows you to listen to the entire argument of a case from start to finish.
- Finally, **Opinion** and **Opinion Announcement** allow you to read the

Court's opinion in these cases and to hear (when available) the announcement of that opinion in open court.

We envisioned this book not only as a source of important commentary, but also as a twenty-first-century tool for the study of the very style and delivery of the oral arguments that have shaped the history of our nation's highest law. We hope you enjoy this book as a combined reading and listening experience.

T.R.J. and J.G.

A Good Quarrel

Introduction

The Role of Oral Arguments in the Supreme Court

TIMOTHY R. JOHNSON AND JERRY GOLDMAN

THE FEDERAL GOVERNMENT PUTS ON MANY IMPRESSIVE DISPLAYS in Washington, D.C. Every four years, the nation inaugurates a president, and hundreds of thousands of people attend various celebratory events. Once a year, Congress invites the president to give an appraisal of the state of the union in front of all senators and representatives, the cabinet, some (or sometimes all) Supreme Court justices, and various other dignitaries. Any day Congress is in session, visitors may obtain passes to sit in the Senate or House galleries to watch our legislative process in action. People may also watch extensive coverage of both houses on C-SPAN. All of these events are witnessed by thousands, hundreds of thousands, or even millions of people each year. In other words, citizens find it relatively easy to see their elected representatives in action, sometimes in person, sometimes on television, or on the Internet.

In contrast, our third branch of government, the U.S. Supreme Court, appears in the public eye less often than does Congress or the president. In fact, while the Court's proceedings for oral arguments are open to the public, far fewer people see the justices in action than see members of either of the other branches. Two factors contribute to this outcome. First, the courtroom has limited available seating. Even those who are lucky enough to witness an oral argument usually only glimpse about three minutes of the give-and-take between attorneys and justices. But in most cases, anyone willing to stand in line will be well rewarded. Of course, in highly salient cases, the lines can be extraordinarily long. In fact, the Court anticipates such occurrences. For example, in *Planned Parenthood of Southeastern Pennsylvania v. Casey* (1992) the Court's public information officer, Toni House, sent a memo to the justices detailing seating arrangements for the gallery. Among other things, only one hundred seats were reserved for the public, and the line for those seats officially formed at midnight the night before the arguments.

Second, the Court simply hears very few cases. While as late as 1992, the justices sat for more than one hundred cases per term, today that number averages fewer than eighty. The courtroom, therefore, is inaccessible for most citizens who make the trek to Washington to experience government in action. In addition, as several of the essays in this volume note, the Court does not videotape its oral arguments or opinion announcements. Thus, even if people wanted to see the Court in action, they could not do so on C-SPAN or on other visual media outlets.

While for each case, an audiotape and written transcription are prepared, neither has historically been much more accessible than the live arguments. Yet the Court has tried to alleviate this problem. Indeed, since the 2006 term, it releases the written transcripts of arguments on the same day they are heard. The release of audio takes longer—these materials are released to the National Archives in the October following the term during which the cases were argued. Authorized vendors then makes copies for use by researchers, a process that often requires an additional few months. Since the Court is now recording its sessions digitally, that lag time should drop from a few months to a few weeks.

The Court has taken one other step toward opening itself to the world. Beginning in December 2000, it has made certain cases more accessible to the public. That is, at the behest of the chief justice, the audio of the oral arguments may be released on the day of the proceedings if heightened public interest warrants such an expedited release. These are not simultaneous (i.e., live) feeds from the courtroom but rather delayed releases within a few hours of the argument. Despite this policy, Chief Justice William H. Rehnquist and Chief Justice John G. Roberts Jr. have taken this action in only a handful of cases, including *Bush v. Gore* (2000), *Boumediene v. Bush* (2008), *Al Odah v. United States* (2008), *Ralph Baze and Thomas C. Bowling, Petitioners v. John D. Rees, Commissioner, Kentucky Department of Corrections, et al.* (2008), *Hamdi v. Rumsfeld* (2004), and *Rumsfeld v. Padilla* (2004).

Despite the fact that far fewer people see the Court in action than watch Congress or the president and despite the slow release of audio recordings of the oral arguments, justices in open court put on a most remarkable—arguably *the* most impressive—display of any of our federal institutions. Even in what the justices themselves might describe as boring or mundane tax cases, the arguments always begin with a bang. At precisely ten o'clock on argument mornings, the justices enter through the red velvet curtains behind the bench, and the marshal rises from his or her station to proclaim:

> The honorable, the chief justice and associate justices of the Supreme Court of the United States. Oyez! Oyez! Oyez! All persons having business before the honorable, the Supreme Court of the United States, are admonished to draw near and give their attention, for the Court is now sitting. God save the United States and this honorable court! 🔊

The pomp and circumstance continues as the chief justice gavels the first case to order. And, in some cases, the fireworks continue throughout the hourlong session.

Because the Court makes its arguments available to the public but so few citizens are able to see or hear these arguments in person, we have sought to bring them to life through commentary by some of the nation's leading Court reporters. We have also linked these commen-

---

To listen to passages from oral arguments indicated with 🔊, visit www.goodquarrel.com.

taries directly to audio recordings of the arguments (available at www.goodquarrel.com).[1] In short, we provide a way for citizens to take fuller advantage of what the Court offers the public so that those who cannot attend arguments can experience what transpires during these proceedings.

Specifically, we take you inside the U.S. Supreme Court's courtroom for several landmark arguments of the last half of the twentieth century and some of the best (and worst) arguments from 1967 to 2006. To do so, we asked a cadre of the nation's most esteemed Court reporters—including Slate.com's Dahlia Lithwick, National Public Radio's Nina Totenberg, the *Los Angeles Times*'s David Savage, and the *Legal Times*'s Tony Mauro—to choose and analyze arguments. This volume takes readers into these cases in an entirely new way. By accessing the Internet, readers can listen to an entire argument while reading commentary from these and other reporters. Readers can also navigate on the Web to the specific sections of the oral arguments that the reporters find particularly interesting, noteworthy, or important.

To place this work in some context, we provide a brief overview of what former and current justices have said about the importance of oral arguments. These comments support our contention that these proceedings are not only interesting but also fundamental to the way the Court decides cases. We then preview the commentators' analyses of some of the best, most interesting, and maybe most forgettable arguments of the past forty years.

Oral Arguments: The Justices Speak

Almost universally, past and present Supreme Court justices view the oral arguments as a fundamental part of their decision-making process (see Johnson 2004). While some dissension from this view exists, Justice Robert H. Jackson summed up the general sentiment: "I think the justices would answer unanimously that now, as traditionally, they rely

1. Jerry Goldman has enabled interested persons to hear thousands of fully digitized oral arguments at http://www.oyez.org. Transcripts are also available so that readers can follow along with many of these arguments.

heavily on oral presentations. . . . [I]t always is of the highest, and often of controlling, importance" (1951, 801). Justice Lewis F. Powell Jr. reaffirmed Jackson's sentiment several decades later: "[T]he fact is, as every judge knows . . . the oral argument . . . does contribute significantly to the development of precedents" (quoted in Stern and Gressman 1993, 571). Other justices agree that these proceedings at times greatly affect decisions (Hughes 1928; White 1982; Rehnquist 2001).

These accounts resemble Justice John Marshall Harlan II's experience with oral arguments at the Court. When he kept a diary of his postargument impressions of a case, Harlan found that "more times than not, the views which I had at the end of the day's session jibed with the final views I formed after the more careful study of the briefs" (1955, 7). More recent justices have supported Harlan's conclusions: Justice William J. Brennan Jr., for example, asserted, "I have had too many occasions when my judgment of a decision has turned on what happened in oral argument" (quoted in Stern and Gressman 1993, 732). He suggested that although this process did not necessarily determine how he voted, it helped him to form his substantive thoughts about a case: "Often my idea of how a case shapes up is changed by oral argument" (quoted in Stern and Gressman 1993, 732). Rehnquist agreed with this assertion and argued that oral advocacy could affect his thoughts about specific cases: "I think that in a significant minority of cases in which I have heard oral argument, I have left the bench feeling different about the case than I did when I came on the bench. The change is seldom a full one-hundred-and-eighty-degree swing" (2001, 243).

Initially, however, not all justices believed that oral arguments were important. Before joining the Court, Justice Antonin G. Scalia, for one, thought them "a dog and pony show"; after almost a decade on the Court, however, he came to believe that "[t]hings can be put in perspective during oral argument in a way that they can't in a written brief" (quoted in O'Brien 2000, 260). Rehnquist agreed: in his words, a good oral argument "will have something to do with how the case comes out" (2001, 244).

While most justices have positive attitudes about the oral arguments, some have at times been disappointed with the quality of advocacy. As Chief Justice Warren E. Burger once observed, "The quality is far below what it could be" (quoted in Stern and Gressman 1993, 571). In fact, Burger moved the Court away from two hours of argument per case (one hour per side) to one hour per case (half an hour per side).[2] Powell too was disappointed at the level of advocacy he saw after joining the Supreme Court: "I certainly had expected that there would be relatively few mediocre performances before the Court. I regret to say that performance has not measured up to my expectations" (quoted in Stern and Gressman 1993, 571). And the quality of argument may compromise one side's ability to win its case.

Why do the justices believe oral arguments are important? Different justices provide different answers to this question. Rehnquist posited that oral arguments allow justices to evaluate counsel's "strong and weak points, and to ask . . . some questions" about the case (1984, 1025). Similarly, Justice Byron R. White suggested that during these proceedings, the Court treats lawyers as resources (1982, 383). That is, counsel come to the Court to provide new or clarifying information that enables the justices to gain a clearer picture of the case at hand. Indeed, there may be points about which the justices remain unclear after reading the briefs, and this face-to-face exchange can clarify such matters. As Rehnquist argued, "One can do his level best to digest from the briefs . . . what he believes necessary to decide the case, and still find himself falling short in one aspect or another of either the law or the facts. Oral argument can cure these shortcomings" (2001, 245).

Justice William O. Douglas held a somewhat different perspective on oral arguments, contending that these proceedings were meant to teach the justices about the key points of a case: "The purpose of a hearing is that the Court may learn what it does not know. . . . It is the education of the Justices . . . that is the essential function of the appellate lawyer" (quoted in Galloway 1989, 84). Moreover, Harlan claimed that oral arguments are the best mechanism for information gathering:

2. Prior to 1969, cases on the Court's summary docket received one hour for arguments (a half hour per side), while regular cases had two hours (one hour per side). Burger permanently abolished the distinction when he took over the Court in 1969 (Rehnquist 2001, 242).

"[T]here is no substitute . . . for the Socratic method of procedure in getting at the real heart of an issue and in finding out where the truth lies" (1955, 7).

As Rehnquist wrote, "Oral argument offers a direct interchange of ideas between court and counsel. . . . Counsel can play a significant role in responding to the concerns of the judges, concerns that counsel won't always be able to anticipate when preparing briefs" (1984, 1021). Thus, he believed oral argument to be "[p]robably the most important catalyst for generating further thought" (2001, 241). In Rehnquist's summation, "Justices of the Supreme Court of the United States have almost unanimously agreed that effective oral advocacy is one of the most powerful tools of the professions" (1986, 289). Even a skeptic such as Scalia changed his view after joining the Court.

A Sneak Preview of the Book

Given the significance that current and former Supreme Court justices place on oral arguments, we believe it is important for the public to better understand what transpires during these proceedings. And who better to provide such insight than the commentators and analysts who follow the Court from the first Monday in October each year until the end of the Court's term the following June? In this volume, eleven of the country's most respected Supreme Court reporters write about an argument of their choice. Some of them chose to assess landmark cases, while others decided to write about what they view as the best oral arguments they witnessed. Finally, others wrote about arguments that were, simply put, not up to the standards of top-notch appellate advocacy. To put each case in context, we provide a short paragraph at the beginning of each chapter that summarizes the key issues in the case. From there, our authors take over to spin their tales from inside the Court.

The first two reporters provide compelling analyses of important cases and give insight into the oral argument process more generally. Dahlia Lithwick focuses on one of the most difficult situations before the Court: a litigant arguing pro se (on his or her own behalf). This case,

Elk Grove Unified School District v. Newdow (2004), takes the reader into Michael Newdow's "rule-breaking" arguments.[3] Specifically, Lithwick shows how in arguing that the justices should strike the words *under God* from the Pledge of Allegiance, Newdow flaunted many of the Court's norms yet still managed to make one of the most effective arguments in years. Lithwick defines the Court's "Ten Commandments of Oral Advocacy," then analyzes how Newdow effectively broke all of them and ultimately lost his case.

Tim O'Brien voyages into the world of white supremacist politics and introduces a litigant who chose to argue even though he had no experience doing so. O'Brien analyzes not only the events preceding the arguments but also the arguments themselves in *Forsyth County, Georgia v. the Nationalist Movement* (1992). While the justices took the Forsyth County attorney to task for defending a law that seemed to quash political speech, the attorney for and chief executive officer of the Nationalist Movement, Richard Barrett, took things to new heights during oral arguments. Whereas Newdow broke almost every courtroom rule and still made a highly effective argument, Barrett's pontification and his sometimes emotional arguments influenced the justices' decision making in ways he did not intend.

Lyle Denniston examines *Planned Parenthood v. Casey* (1992), the controlling precedent in abortion law. He reveals how the interchange of attorneys and justices affected the outcome of this case. In particular, the questions asked by and responses to Justices Sandra Day O'Connor and Anthony M. Kennedy highlight their concerns about undercutting the existing precedent in *Roe v. Wade* (1973) as well as about the standard the Court should set for abortion law in the United States.

Charles Bierbauer takes a new look at the arguments from possibly the most significant case of the new century, *Bush v. Gore* (2000), analyzing the justices' only public interactions with one another on the matter. Specifically, he points out that the justices spent a good deal of time discussing jurisdictional issues. Bierbauer also highlights a key

3. The Supreme Court has explicit and implicit guidelines for how attorneys should act when appearing before the Court. All attorneys try to follow these guidelines, and many read Stern, Gressman, and Shapiro 2007, which is regarded as the Bible for advocates appearing before our nation's highest court.

faux pas made by many attorneys—calling justices by the wrong names. Finally, through recent interviews about the arguments, Bierbauer draws out how the attorneys viewed what transpired when they appeared before the justices.

Tony Mauro begins his analysis of *Glickman v. Wileman Brothers and Elliott Inc.* (1997) several months before the argument. He goes behind the scenes of an intense debate about which attorney should represent Wileman Brothers in the oral arguments at the U.S. Supreme Court. The resolution of this debate provides for fascinating reading, and as Mauro concludes, Wileman Brothers was so incensed with the choice of attorneys and with the "raucous" nature of his arguments that the company took drastic action shortly after the Court handed down its final decision.

Greg Stohr focuses on another case remarkable for both its content and its high level of advocacy, *Grutter v. Bollinger* (2003). First, Stohr expounds on the incredible amount of time attorneys spend preparing for the intense questioning they will face from the justices. He also points out how attorneys can dig themselves into holes at the beginning of an argument and how justices will sometimes come to the rescue. This analysis demonstrates the dividends of preparation. Indeed, the better-prepared attorney can often win a case at oral arguments.

As Bierbauer and Mauro note, oral arguments certainly at times do not measure up to the quality justices have come to expect. Nina Totenberg analyzes a "truly wretched" argument in *Chandler v. Miller* (1997). Not only was Chandler torn apart almost from the beginning of his argument, but he was so unprepared for the onslaught of questions that he "had the aura of a sleepwalker." While other chapters in this volume demonstrate how one or two justices can decimate one side's argument, this case exemplifies how thoroughly the entire Court, from Justice Scalia to Justice O'Connor to Justice Ruth Bader Ginsburg, can collectively tear an attorney limb from limb. The justices were equally harsh toward Georgia's assistant attorney general, Patricia Guilday, whom Totenberg describes as having "self-immolate[d]."

David Savage writes about *Rapanos v. United States* (2006), which concerned the federal government's control of navigable waterways. This case is historic for many reasons, not the least of which is that it was the first oral argument for newly appointed Associate Justice Samuel A. Alito Jr., who had won confirmation to the Court less than a month earlier. Savage notes that even though Alito was the newest justice, he reached the heart of the problem with *Rapanos*'s argument. This chapter more generally highlights how attorneys deal with questions—sometimes difficult and harsh ones—from all members of the bench. Savage also draws out the stark differences in the questioning styles of Justices Scalia and Stevens.

Brent Kendall's analysis of *Randall v. Sorrell* (2006) follows. Using this campaign finance case from Vermont, Kendall demonstrates that the justices often send signals about how they will rule in the case by the frequency of their questions and by asking questions of the attorneys for one side or the other. He notes that Randall's attorney argued for a full three minutes before a justice raised a question, an unusual occurrence because the justices usually dominate the arguments. The second signal was the change in "pace and energy" as Sorrell reached the lectern for his argument—in particular, the questioning by Chief Justice Roberts.

Steve Lash provides insight into *UAAAIWA v. Johnson Controls Inc.* (1991), a case focusing on whether women have the right to choose to work under hazardous conditions even when pregnant. He provides evidence that on some occasions, everything and everyone involved in the case click perfectly. Given the high level of advocacy as well as the high level of engaging questions from the bench, this case offers a quintessential instructional example for civics classes, classes on appellate advocacy, or constitutional law classes.

We close with Fred Graham's analysis of *Time Inc. v. Hill* (1967). This case was significant for the legal standard it set: any story "in the public interest" may be published, even if it concerns private citizens. The case was also interesting because of what transpired nine months before the Court handed down its ruling. Indeed, the oral arguments included soon-to-be presidential candidate Richard M. Nixon. The most intriguing parts of this argument are the interchanges among Nixon, an outspoken conservative, and the liberal wing of the Court, including Justice Abe Fortas and Chief Justice Earl Warren.

Elk Grove Unified School District v. Newdow

Ten Commandments of Oral Arguments

ARGUED MARCH 24, 2004

DAHLIA LITHWICK

Michael Newdow's daughter attended public school in the Elk Grove Unified School District in California. Elk Grove teachers began school days by leading students in a voluntary recitation of the Pledge of Allegiance, including the words under God, *added by a 1954 congressional act. Newdow sued in federal district court in California, arguing that making students listen—even if they choose not to participate—to the words* under God *violates the Establishment Clause of the U.S. Constitution's First Amendment. The U.S. Ninth Circuit Court of Appeals held that Newdow had standing "to challenge a practice that interferes with his right to direct the religious education of his daughter." It also ruled that both Congress's 1954 act adding the words* under God *to the Pledge and the school district policy requiring that the Pledge be recited violated the First Amendment's Establishment Clause.*

To listen to passages from oral arguments indicated with 🔊, visit www.goodquarrel.com.

WATCHING JUST A HANDFUL OF ORAL ARGUMENTS AT THE U.S. Supreme Court quickly leads to the recognition that only a few immutable rules of the road exist, separating the truly outstanding oral advocates from the really terrible ones. A small cadre of attorneys—the Supreme Court's Harlem Globetrotters—argues the vast majority of the high-profile cases at the high court. This group of lawyers frequently mops up the Court with the earnest criminal defense attorneys, overworked state attorneys general, and well-meaning trial lawyers who have shepherded their cases all the way up from the lower courts. It's not that the Harlem Globetrotters are smarter or better lawyers than their opponents. It's simply that ordinary attorneys haven't always been instructed in the very different rules that apply on Maryland Avenue. These aren't rules about the briefing schedule. These are the rules of how to persuade nine grumpy old justices.

The best oral advocates seem to have memorized and internalized these rules: You don't get emotional or overwrought in laying out your case; you don't bore the justices with a tear-jerking narrative; you don't betray your suspicion that you're smarter than the justices (even when you are); and you never, ever try to be funnier than they are (even when you can be). Perhaps most urgently, you never become so invested in some matter of national legal concern—particularly one that involves a member of your own family—that you get yourself admitted to the Supreme Court bar for the sole purpose of arguing your own case. All this advice boils down into a single immutable commandment: There is no room for a tenth ego at the U.S. Supreme Court.

That's what made oral argument in *Elk Grove Unified School District v. Newdow* (2004)[1] the biggest surprise for Court-watchers that year. It also made *Newdow*—widely known as the Pledge of Allegiance case—one of the most instructive oral arguments I've ever watched. Not because Michael Newdow—who argued the case, as he had done at every court since the first motions were filed—followed all the rules about how to conduct himself at the marble temple. Somehow, he performed brilliantly even as he broke virtually every one of those rules. True, the case ultimately was not resolved in his favor. But despite the

1. 542 U.S. 1.

fact he seemingly did everything wrong, he managed to wow the spectators, charm the press, and even—although I doubt they would ever admit it—impress most of the justices. So, on the theory that sometimes you learn more from the rule breakers than the followers, here's a walk through the Newdow argument.

Argued on March 24, 2004, the case promised to be a train wreck. Michael Newdow is one of those smartest-kids-in-class guys, the man who somehow manages to rub everyone—even his greatest admirers—the wrong way. Newdow is a physician who attended law school but never practiced law. He was disputing the constitutionality of the words *under God* in the Pledge of Allegiance, arguing that they violated the First Amendment's ban on entangling church and state. The trigger for his outrage was that his young daughter was being pressured to recite the pledge at her public school, a space in which the courts have traditionally been particularly anxious about any hint of religious coercion. Newdow, who had no staff or paralegals and didn't even take the bar exam until 2002, filed his action and argued it all the way up through the Ninth Circuit Court of Appeals, where he prevailed on most of his claims. The nation went crazy, and the Supreme Court agreed to hear the matter. Newdow, not surprisingly, planned to argue it there as well.

Long before Newdow darkened the Court's marble halls, magazine and newspaper profiles revealed him to be the antithesis of the silver-tongued hired guns that usually argue such major cases. The advocate was pushy and self-justifying, emotionally overinvolved, seemingly incapable of separating his fury over an ugly custody battle with the child's mother from the constitutional merits of the dispute, and brash in a way one simply never sees at the Court (with the exception of certain justices). Within seconds of his argument, it was abundantly clear that he was not going to play by any of the Court's genteel rules of conduct. Newdow was a barroom brawler, and he made no apology for it.

Among the many, many unspoken laws of oral advocacy shattered by Newdow that day, the following were only the most notable.

1. *Thou Shalt Not Insult the Integrity of the Judiciary in Advance of Oral Argument.* Even before he showed his face at the Court, Newdow shocked Court watchers and even the justices themselves by filing

an almost unheard-of motion seeking the recusal of Justice Antonin G. Scalia based on the justice's public remarks before hearing the case. Newdow not only overtly and publicly questioned Scalia's ability to hear the case impartially but also succeeded in getting the usually intransigent justice to stay off the case ("Scalia Attacks" 2003).

2. *Thou Shalt Not Make a Play for Judicial Heartstrings That Are Not in Evidence.* The first sentence out of Newdow's mouth was both personal and emotional.

> Every school morning in the Elk Grove Unified School District's public schools, government agents, teachers, funded with tax dollars, have their students stand up, including my daughter, face the flag of the United States of America, place their hands over their hearts, and affirm that ours is a nation under some particular religious entity, the appreciation of which is not accepted by numerous people, such as myself. . . . I am an atheist. I don't believe in God. And every school morning my child is asked to stand up, face that flag, put her hand over her heart, and say that her father is wrong.

This is an astonishing opening in many ways. He isn't telling the Court what the constitutional dispute means to them or to the nation; he is describing, in completely personal terms, how it affects him and his relationship with his *child,* of all things. The Court usually shuts down this sort of emotionalism in a second. Yet within moments, he was interrupted by Justice Anthony M. Kennedy, seeking to address Newdow's standing to bring suit. What was amazing was that Kennedy phrased the standing question in the most personal terms as well: "It seems to me these aren't just technical rules that we lawyers are interested in, but that there's a common-sense component to it. . . . It seems to me that your daughter is—is the one that bears the blame for this. She's going to face the public outcry."

It is also unusual at oral argument to hear the justices fretting about the ruling's effect on a party, even if that party is a child. He privileges concern for that child over the "technical rules." Kennedy is making a larger point here about Newdow's standing to sue. But he is less concerned with standing than with negative publicity, which is not a legal issue in and of itself. This is rather tenderhearted language, especially coming from this particular bench.

And Newdow's response is quite deft: He tells Kennedy that "harms that occur as the result of prejudices of our society" are not a sound basis for ignoring a constitutional wrong. It is as if he is telling the justice, "This is personal to me, but you should focus on the constitutional problems, please."

3. *Thou Shalt Not Describe the Parties in the Case in Reference to Thine Own Self.* The words *I* and *mine* are as anathema to most oral advocates as they are staples of small children. All of the best Supreme Court attorneys know that the justices don't much care what the attorneys think and don't want to hear what they want or how the case will affect them personally. The justices care about the following things, ranked in declining order of importance: (1) the Constitution; (2) the Court; (3) not looking stupid; (4) not overtly overruling anything; (5) the dignity of states; (6) the dignity of the parties; (7) what they are going to eat for dinner; (8) what the oral advocates want.

For these reasons, most attorneys presenting oral arguments do not talk about themselves or their stake in the litigation. Granted, Newdow was somewhat unusual in that he in fact had a very personal stake in this litigation; this was, after all, his child. But anyone advising him prior to oral argument would have urged him to argue this case on its constitutional merits alone. Those suggestions clearly would have fallen on deaf ears. And the extent to which Newdow kept reminding the Court of his investment in the outcome was quite amazing and—counterintuitively—very effective. When Kennedy made it clear that he believed Newdow's interests and his daughter's interests diverged and that he wasn't sure whether Newdow had standing on his own, Newdow's reply was unequivocal: "I am saying [that] I as her father have a right to know that when she goes into the public schools, she's not going to be told every morning to be asked to stand up, put her hand over her heart, and say 'Your father is wrong.' . . . That is an actual, concrete, discrete, particularized, individualized harm to me."

4. *Thou Shalt Not Be Combative with the Justices.* In the normal, garden-variety oral argument, oral advocates push back at the justices only very gently. In the most extreme cases, someone will say something like, "Respectfully, I disagree." But not Michael Newdow. His willingness to let the justices know the precise depth and width of their wrongness knew almost no bounds. When Justice Ruth Bader Ginsburg observed that "there is another custodian of this child who makes the final decision who doesn't agree with you," Newdow's response teetered right on the border of rude: "Well, first of all, I'm not convinced about her making the final decision. I think it was shown when I tried to get my child to attend the Ninth Circuit that she certainly does *not* have the final decision-making power. She has a temporary final decision-making power which is good for about three days until we get to Court." It's not totally clear what "temporary final decision-making power" even means as a legal matter, but it certainly sounded convincing.

5. *Thou Shalt Not Suggest That Thou Art Smarter Than Thine Justices.* Newdow went to the mat with Justice Kennedy over whether the Pledge of Allegiance can be characterized as a prayer, similar to the prayer in *Lee v. Weisman* (1992),[2] which barred "coercive" religious prayer at a school graduation. Kennedy wrote the decision in that case, yet in *Elk Grove,* Newdow almost scolded the justice about what constitutes coercion under the Establishment Clause. When Kennedy observed, "One is a prayer, the other isn't," Newdow responded, "Again. The Establishment Clause does not require a prayer. To put the Ten Commandments on the wall was not a prayer, yet this Court said that violated the Establishment Clause. To teach evolution or not teach evolution doesn't involve prayer. But that can violate the Establishment Clause!" Newdow took another whack at Kennedy later in the argument, claiming near the end that although he believes that the Pledge is a "religious exercise," "whether or not you do or I do [believe it] is somewhat, I think, irrelevant." It's not often that you hear an attorney tell a justice that what he thinks is "irrelevant." I generally wouldn't suggest doing so. But Newdow somehow pulled it off.

2. 505 U.S. 577.

6. *Thou Shalt Not Wax Metaphysical with Thine Justices.* Justice Stephen G. Breyer is a notorious pragmatist, forever searching for a way to bridge the divide between the parties to the case and the Court. Newdow rebuffed the justice's attempt to reach out a conciliatory hand, as Breyer seemed to anticipate. He prefaced his question with, "I think the answer's gonna be 'no,' but . . ." before asking whether Newdow could find a place in his heart for an inclusive "set of beliefs—sincere beliefs—which in any ordinary person's life fills the same place as a belief in God fills in the life of an orthodox religionist. So it's reaching out to be inclusive, maybe to include you." Newdow replies, "I don't think that I can include *under God* to mean no God, which is exactly what I think. I deny the existence of God, and for someone to tell me that *under God* should mean some broad thing that even encompasses my religious beliefs sounds a little, you know, it sounds like the government is imposing what it wants me to think in terms of religion." There wasn't much left for Breyer to say after that.

7. *Thou Shalt Not Use Multiplex-Grade Sound Effects When Appearing before the Justices.* Oral advocates, don't try this at home. In attempting to explain why the words *under God* are not meaningless or "under the constitutional radar" for an atheist, Newdow arguably goes over the top: "When I see the flag and I think of pledging allegiance, it's like I'm getting slapped in the face every time. BAM!" Yet somehow, when Newdow spoke these words, he conveyed to the Court the degree of his outrage at the words *under God* in the Pledge.

8. *Thou Shalt Not Seek Perfection in the Law.* No veteran Supreme Court lawyer would have bickered with Justice Breyer when he stated that the Pledge is "not perfect, but it serves a purpose of unification at the price of offending a small number of people like you." But Newdow revealed himself to be a constitutional romantic with his rejoinder, which really was just about perfect: "For sixty-two years, the Pledge did serve its purpose of unification, and it did so perfectly. It didn't include some religious dogma that separated out some. . . . The Pledge of Allegiance . . . got us through two world wars, got us through the depres-

sion, got us through everything without God, and then Congress stuck God in there for that particular reason."

9. *Thou Shalt Not Break up the Crowd in Uproarious Laughter, Especially at the Expense of the Chief Justice.* The absolute high point of oral argument came when Newdow made the crowd laugh harder than did Chief Justice William H. Rehnquist. Rehnquist landed a solid punch when he asked Newdow what the vote was in Congress when it incorporated the words *under God* into the Pledge. Newdow replied that the vote was unanimous, and Rehnquist cracked, "Well, that doesn't sound divisive," causing the gallery to burst out laughing. Not content to let the chief have his moment, Newdow cut him off: "That's only because no atheist can get elected to public office! The studies show that 48 percent of the population cannot get elected." At which point the laughter turned to boisterous clapping, a sound I have heard neither before nor since at the Court. And while the chief justice was visibly annoyed—he promptly threatened to clear the courtroom in the event of any more clapping—the justices seemed not to hold the incident against Newdow.

10. *Thou Shalt Not Cite Extralegal Sources.* Newdow was the first oral advocate I've seen cite newspapers and opinion columns as frequently as the Constitution. Most lawyers stick to the fiction that the justices are too busy sipping sherry and reading hornbooks to care what the world thinks. Responding to a question from Justice John Paul Stevens about whether the words *under God* have the same meaning to the country today as they did when they were inserted into the Pledge, Newdow offered an amazingly effective response: "I would merely note that ninety-nine out of ninety-nine senators stopped what they were doing and went out on the front steps of the Capitol to say that they want *under God* there. The president of the United States in a press conference with Vladimir Putin decided the first thing he was going to talk about was this decision. It was on the front page of every newspaper. This was supposed to be one of the major cases of this Court's term." It may be unorthodox to cite to the world outside the courthouse, but doing so certainly conveyed Newdow's point that people want the words *under God* to be retained.

Finally, Newdow somehow managed to time his conclusion perfectly, like an Olympic skater landing a triple lutz. Most oral advocates run out of time or finish abruptly in midsentence. But Newdow somehow managed to close exactly as his half hour ran out: "There's a principle here, and I'm hoping the Court will uphold this principle so that we can finally go back and have every American want to stand up, face the flag, place their hand over their heart, and pledge to one nation, indivisible—not divided by religion—with liberty and justice for all."

Newdow did not prevail on his claims, although his loss on the question of standing certainly left the door open for future challenges (which Newdow has spearheaded). But to my mind, the enduring lesson of *Elk Grove* is the same lesson taught by just about every movie about a rebellious teenage football player/dancer/spelling bee competitor/ science fair participant: sometimes, the outsider, with all his rough edges and miscues, can prevail over the smooth polish of the insider, not because he knows all the rules but because his passion to win is greater than the sum of those rules.

Forsyth County, Georgia v. the Nationalist Movement

A Workman-like Performance

ARGUED MARCH 31, 1992

TIM O'BRIEN

Forsyth County's Ordinance 34 mandated that all persons seeking to engage in private demonstrations must obtain a permit. It also declared that participants in demonstrations should bear the cost of protection because such activities often go beyond the normal cost of law enforcement. Third, the ordinance required permit applicants to pay a fee up to one thousand dollars. Finally, it empowered the county administrator to adjust the fee to meet the expense of maintaining public order. The Nationalist Movement sued when the county imposed a fee for its proposed demonstration in opposition to Martin Luther King Jr. Day. The court of appeals held that an ordinance that charges more than a nominal fee for using public forums for public issue speech is unconstitutional.

To listen to passages from oral arguments indicated with 🔊, visit www.goodquarrel.com.

ORAL ARGUMENT IN THE U.S. SUPREME COURT IS THE THINKING person's spectator sport, and a grand one at that. Brilliant lawyers are occasionally reduced to a very small size, while fools can be enlarged beyond any reasonable measure, all in the service of justice. Most cases involve complicated application of the U.S. Constitution or federal statutes. To those unfamiliar with the background of a case, the arguments in Court may be all but incomprehensible. And in most cases, there really is no right answer. The Constitution sets the jurisdiction of the Court, and its proceedings are subject to federal regulation and internal Court rules. But as any Supreme Court observer will tell you, the most revered rule at the Court is the so-called Rule of Five. That is, the correct answer is whatever gets five votes. And what might get five votes can change, often because the Court has changed, occasionally because the Court has found that the country itself has changed, or, as the justices might put it, "[T]he evolving standards of decency that mark the progress of a maturing society" have changed.[1]

Supreme Court advocates are ill-advised to equate their abilities with their won-lost records. Yet oral argument is important. It can affect the scope of a decision or a dissent, and it accords the justices their only meaningful opportunity to communicate with one another. (Contrary to popular opinion, they don't really debate the cases at their weekly conferences, only vote on them.) In fact, Justice John Paul Stevens has been known occasionally to borrow the recordings of oral argument and listen to them in his car on the way home from Court. Evidence from the academy also shows that these proceedings may affect case outcomes (see, e.g., Wasby, D'Amato, and Metrailer 1976; Johnson 2004; Johnson, Spriggs, and Wahlbreck 2007). While a good argument might on rare occasions turn the Court around, other factors beyond the advocate's control are much more dispositive, such as the inherent merits of the case and whether the argument presented happens to coincide with the evolving attitudes of the Court's members.

There is no adequate handbook on precisely how to argue before the high court, but advocates often begin with the "Supreme Court Bible"

1. *Trop v. Dulles,* 356 U.S. 86 (1958).

(Stern, Gressman, and Shapiro 2007). The gaffes are much more memorable and often every bit as instructive. So it was in the case of *Forsyth County, Georgia v. the Nationalist Movement* (1992).[2]

Rural Forsyth County, about thirty miles northeast of Atlanta, has a troubled racial history.[3] In a single month in 1912, its entire African American population—more than a thousand citizens—was systematically driven from the county in the wake of the rape and murder of a white woman and the lynching of her accused assailant. Seventy-five years later, the county remained 99 percent white. Spurred by this history, Hosea Williams, an Atlanta city councilman and civil rights leader, proposed a Forsyth County "March against Fear and Intimidation" for January 17, 1987 (Martin Luther King Jr. Day).

The march initially wasn't much. Only about ninety civil rights demonstrators showed up to parade in Cumming, the county seat. The demonstrators were met, however, by more than four hundred counter-demonstrators, including members of the Ku Klux Klan, who lined the parade route shouting racial slurs. The confrontation quickly degenerated into a rock- and bottle-throwing melee, forcing an end to the parade.

Not to be deterred, Williams planned a return march for the following weekend. The event developed into the largest civil rights demonstration in the South since the 1960s. More than twenty thousand marchers joined the civil rights leaders; roughly a thousand counter-demonstrators were contained by more than three thousand state and local police and National Guardsmen. The police protection cost more than $670,000, none of it paid by the demonstrators; the good citizens of Georgia picked up the tab. The Forsyth County Board of Commissioners needed only three days to respond with Ordinance 34, whose constitutionality would soon reach the nation's highest court.

Ordinance 34 required that any group obtain a permit before using any public property, including streets, for parades or demonstrations. The measure also required every applicant to "pay in advance for such permit, for the use of the County, a sum not more than $1000 for each

2. 505 U.S. 123.

3. From the Court's opinion, 505 U.S. 125.

day such parade, procession, or open air public meeting shall take place." The ordinance was amended on June 8, 1987, to provide for this fee arrangement. Finally, the county administrator was empowered to "adjust the amount to be paid in order to meet the expense incident to the administration of the Ordinance and to the maintenance of public order in the matter licensed."

While Ordinance 34 may have appeared directed at Hosea Williams and other civil rights activists, an activist group of an entirely different stripe sought to challenge the measure as a violation of the First Amendment's guarantee of freedom of speech and assembly. The Nationalist Movement is a loosely knit white separatist organization based in Learned, Mississippi. It proposed a rally on the courthouse steps in Cumming in opposition to the federal holiday commemorating the birthday of Martin Luther King Jr. The county imposed a one-hundred-dollar fee, which did not include any calculation for expenses incurred by law enforcement. Rather, the fee was based on the time spent by the county administrator (put at ten hours) in issuing the permit. The Nationalist Movement did not pay the fee and did not hold the rally. Instead, it brought suit in the U.S. District Court for the Northern District of Georgia, seeking an injunction prohibiting the county from interfering with the Movement's plans.

The District Court upheld the ordinance, finding that the fees were based solely on content-neutral criteria—that is, the actual costs incurred investigating and processing the application. A panel of the U.S. Court of Appeals for the Eleventh Circuit disagreed, finding that "any ordinance which charges more than a nominal fee for using public forums for public issue speech violates the First Amendment."[4] The Court of Appeals then voted to rehear the case en banc (that is, with all of the court's justices sitting). After further briefing, the circuit court reinstated the panel decision in its entirety.[5] The county appealed to the U.S. Supreme Court, which agreed to hear the case on September 27, 1991.

4. 913 F.2d 895 (1990).

5. 934 F.2d 1482 (1991).

The case was set for oral argument on March 31, 1992. Our reporting style at ABC News was to get whatever background video we could of Supreme Court cases, including interviews with those most directly involved in the case. While many cases involve exalted principles of constitutional law, all of them also involve human beings with real, personal stakes in the outcome. The background video was extremely important for television and helped "humanize" these often-difficult but nonetheless important conflicts. Getting file video of the demonstrations in Forsyth County was not a problem. Not only did the ABC affiliate have lots of it, the demonstrations—particularly the racist taunting at the initial civil rights demonstration—had made national news, and ABC News's tape library contained ample video. Getting video of the Nationalist Movement and its leaders turned out to be substantially more problematic. The Movement is headquartered in rural Mississippi, about thirty miles west of Jackson. The attorney of record on the brief was Richard Barrett, who, it turns out, was also the group's chief executive officer. The organization did not appear to have any formal offices, and Barrett could not identify how many members it had. It apparently is a small group with extreme white supremacist views. Rather than travel to Learned, I set up an on-camera interview with Barrett on the steps of the Supreme Court at five o'clock on March 30, the eve of his argument.

I'm not sure what I was expecting in Richard Barrett, but, whatever it was, it wasn't what I got. He was a large, bearlike man with a warm smile and a friendly—even jovial—demeanor. We quickly got down to business because in taped television interviews, I have found it a bad idea to warm up the interviewee. The person inevitably will tell you everything, coherently and passionately, up front and then go dead when the camera is turned on. Here, Barrett explained his opposition to a holiday for Martin Luther King Jr., whom Barrett simply felt was undeserving. King, Barrett contended, had done more to undermine the rights of white folks than to advance the rights of black folks.

Cutting to the chase, I suggested that perhaps he felt he had been discriminated against because of the Movement's minority (ahem) views. He agreed. If he was marching in favor of something less controversial—say, motherhood—the permit, at least in theory, might be less expensive, right? Continuing, I suggested that the fee should be the same whether you're marching in favor of motherhood, abortion, or gay rights. I did not think that this was a difficult question, but I was taken aback by Barrett's answer. "Oh no. It's not the same. You can't make that comparison!" "Because?" "Because abortion and homosexuality violate God's law, and that's even superior to constitutional law." Barrett went on to explain how advocates of abortion rights or gay rights should not receive a permit at all.

He didn't stop there. When the interview ended, Barrett asked if I thought Justice Clarence Thomas would participate. Five months earlier, Thomas had assumed the seat of retiring Justice Thurgood Marshall, a civil rights pioneer and the Court's first black justice. Did Barrett feel that Thomas, as the Court's only sitting African American, could not view the dispute objectively but that Thomas's white colleagues could? No, that wasn't it. Rather, Barrett believed that African Americans should be barred from any position of responsibility in the government, that the *Dred Scott* decision[6] was wrong, and that any fair reading of the Bible would clearly so demonstrate. This was the lawyer who, the next morning, would be arguing a potentially landmark First Amendment case in the U.S. Supreme Court. Before we headed our separate ways that evening, Barrett asked if I had any final advice. Sure. He should feign a heart attack, seek a postponement, and hire someone else to do his bidding. I kept these suggestions to myself.

That night, I read the lower court opinions in Barrett's case to learn that he had been barred from further appearances in the district court as a result of having made what the court found to be fraudulent representations. Among Barrett's apparent transgressions, on the morning of one hearing, he appointed a Movement member "acting secretary" to enable him to serve as a witness who could authenticate Movement records. The witness had no knowledge of the records, could not identify them, and had never even seen them until presented them in court that morning. Barrett had also sought to present himself as solely the

6. 60 U.S. 393 (1857).

Movement's counsel, concealing his own personal interest in the outcome of the case. In actuality, Barrett had a leading role in promoting and participating in Movement demonstrations. The trial judge noted that Barrett had been observed in television news reports "standing on the back of a pickup truck with a bullhorn and whipping up the crowds in Forsyth County in the parade."[7]

Concealing or misrepresenting facts is a serious offense for a practicing lawyer. Such misconduct can result in contempt proceedings by the court and/or disciplinary action by the state bar. Courts have held that individuals have a constitutional right to represent themselves at trial, generally without regard to ability or legal training. That, however, is not so in the U.S. Supreme Court, where the impact of a case ordinarily goes far beyond the interests of the parties. Thus, the justices could conceivably have replaced Barrett and appointed outside counsel to defend the lower court's decision in the Movement's favor.

Per Court ritual, at about nine o'clock on the morning of oral arguments, the lawyers presenting their cases will gather in the Lawyers' Conference Room to be briefed by Bill Suter, the amiable Clerk of the Court, about procedure, basic rules, and formalities. In Rehnquist's day, Suter would make it a point to alert the lawyers that Rehnquist preferred to be addressed as "Chief Justice," and not merely "Justice" (On occasion, when an advocate would get it wrong, Rehnquist would consume the lawyer's precious time by explaining the difference and how his elevation to Chief Justice required a separate confirmation hearing.) According to lawyers present during this particular session, Barrett had advised the clerk that he would not be answering any questions put to him by Clarence Thomas but that—consistent with his white supremacist views—he would stand mute, and then move on with his argument. The Court was on notice.

This was not *Roe v. Wade, Bush v. Gore,* or any precedent-setting affirmative action case. But it was nevertheless an important case. And the stage had clearly been set for an interesting morning.

---

7. Cited in 913 F.2d 885, 993.

10:10 A.M., March 31, 1992. Chief Justice William Rehnquist: "We'll hear arguments first this morning in Case 91-538, *Forsyth County, Georgia v. the Nationalist Movement*. Mr. Stubbs."

The Forsyth County attorney, Robert Stubbs, representing the appellant, was first up. Stubbs quickly got to the heart of his argument: the Eleventh U.S. Circuit Court of Appeals had incorrectly invalidated Forsyth County's parade statute by applying the wrong precedent, *Murdock v. Pennsylvania* (1943),[8] when it should have relied on *Cox v. New Hampshire* (1941).[9]

In *Murdock v. Pennsylvania,* the Court threw out the conviction of a Jehovah's Witness for distributing religious pamphlets and soliciting donations without first obtaining a license that cost $1.50 per day or $7.00 per week. The justices concluded that spreading one's beliefs "could be crushed and closed out by the sheer weight of the toll or tribute which is exacted town by town, village by village."[10] Because preferred First Amendment rights were at stake, the most the Constitution might allow (under *Murdock*) would be "a nominal [fee] imposed as a regulatory measure and calculated to defray the expense of protecting those on the streets against the abuse of solicitors."[11] The Eleventh Circuit had read *Murdock* to allow Forsyth County to exact a fee, but only a nominal one, and the court concluded that a fee of up to $1,000.00 in 1989 in Georgia was no more nominal than a fee of $1.50 was in Pennsylvania in 1943.

In *Cox v. New Hampshire,* however, the Court had upheld an ordinance requiring parade permits where official discretion was limited exclusively to considerations of time, place, and manner. Nor did any fee, in the county's view, have to be nominal. County attorney Stubbs noted that with regard to licensing fees, the *Cox* Court said that such fees could have "a permissible range from $300 to a nominal amount, a recognition we believe that indicates there is a difference between $300 and a nomi-

8. 319 U.S. 105.

9. 312 U.S. 569.

10. 319 U.S. 115 (1943).

11. 319 U.S. 115 (1943).

nal amount in 1941." Accordingly, urged Stubbs, the Eleventh Circuit was incorrect to rule that only nominal fees could be allowed.

The argument seemed to work up to that point, but Stubbs went further. He reminded the Court that Article IV, Section 3 of the Constitution "grants Congress, and I quote, 'the power to make all needful rules and regulations respecting property belonging to it.'" Stubbs continued, "The Tenth Amendment reserves to the States those powers not otherwise taken away from them by the Constitution, and this Court in *Cox* stated basically that it was undoubted that there is authority in local government to control the use of its property." It went downhill from there.

Justice Antonin G. Scalia asked, "Mr. Stubbs, that goes a little far, doesn't it? I mean, can the county charge me for jumping up on a soapbox and just all by myself giving a speech, not causing any interference with traffic, not requiring any policeman?" Stubbs tried to explain that that was not how the Forsyth County ordinance worked, but Scalia was not convinced: "But that is the *principle* you were arguing. You were arguing property rights, it seems to me, that just on the basis that it owns the property, the state, despite the First Amendment, can charge. That doesn't seem to me right."

Justice Sandra Day O'Connor jumped in and got Stubbs to acknowledge that there were clear problems associated with whether groups could receive waivers to exempt them from the fee.

JUSTICE O'CONNOR: Now, do you think that the Constitution requires the county to make any exception for indigents and those who are unable to pay a fee?

MR. STUBBS: Yes, ma'am, we believe that, and we do—

JUSTICE O'CONNOR: Do you think that this ordinance does that when it doesn't extend it to a group that has no assets?

While the Nationalist Movement claimed that its total assets amounted to around ninety dollars, O'Connor went on to draw out that under the ordinance, the county's indigence exception applied only to individuals, not organizations. She then inquired, "So if the group organizing a particular gathering on the public streets in Forsyth County wanted to get a permit, you would want an affidavit of indigency from every person participating, is that it?" Stubbs's response spelled trouble for him: "[U]nder the terms of our ordinance, that is what we are stuck with until we can get back and fix it."

Blood in the water. Justice Anthony M. Kennedy smelled it.

JUSTICE KENNEDY: What is the principle upon which you base your conclusion that there must be an indigent waiver? Why don't the rich have an equal right to speech?

After considerable sparring with Justices Kennedy and Scalia, Stubbs confessed that he wasn't sure that the Constitution required an indigence exception for parade permits, but Forsyth County had one anyway, however ambiguous.

It is basic but nonetheless crucial for lawyers arguing before the Court to remember that the principles they ask the Court to adopt will be applied in many other circumstances, a concept never lost on the justices. At this point in the argument, Justice David H. Souter exposed (what seemed to me as) the greatest constitutional infirmities in the Forsyth County ordinance. Souter was troubled that the county's sliding scale fee, based at least in part on what it might cost the county to police the event, might have the unhealthy effect of filtering out those with unpopular or otherwise controversial messages.

JUSTICE SOUTER: So, that on your view, you could have had an ordinance that would have allowed you to charge seven hundred thousand dollars for the civil rights demonstrations or parades in the earlier instances?

MR. STUBBS: Our ordinance puts a cap—

JUSTICE SOUTER: I know *yours* does, but your principle would allow you to do that, is that correct?

MR. STUBBS: Our principle would, Justice Souter.

The discussion continued for a few moments with Stubbs arguing—unconvincingly—that the Forsyth statute was content neutral and merely restricted the time, place, and manner of speech.

Justice Scalia watched, occasionally glancing around the room. He does that. His mind seemed elsewhere. This is a perhaps little-known idiosyncrasy of the justice, but it is usually a perilous foreboding. Scalia is known for wry wit and sharp questions during argument. His silence is often a harbinger—he's about to hone in. And for the hapless lawyer appearing before him, it often means Scalia's wheels are turning—and yours are about to come off.

JUSTICE SCALIA: Mr. Stubbs, am I correct that you not only did not charge for the police protection which you were authorized to charge for, but you didn't even charge the full amount of the administrative costs?

MR. STUBBS: That's correct, Your Honor.

JUSTICE SCALIA: You reduced what it might have been.

MR. STUBBS: The administrator made a determination that he wanted to charge what had been charged the year before so that there would be no—

JUSTICE SCALIA: That is very generous of him. I mean, can he pick which organizations he decides to be generous with? I mean, would he have been as generous if this were a Communist Party demonstration or some other group? What kind of an ordinance is that, anyway?

MR. STUBBS: I think the generosity was an attempt to avoid what has happened, to coming up here, and not out of agreement with the message by any means.

JUSTICE SCALIA: Well, how do we know that? I should think you have to charge all groups on some fixed basis and not—you make the point in your brief as though it is a point in your favor that you didn't charge the full amount that could have been charged. I don't take it as a point in your favor. It is one of the things I worry about with this ordinance, that it allows people to scale the fees as they wish.

To the lay observer, it appeared that Stubbs and the Forsyth County ordinance were in deep trouble. I thought Stubbs had acquitted himself reasonably well, given the difficult hand he had to play. The justices appeared skeptical, but they did not beat Stubbs up as they have with other lawyers who make larger mistakes, such as not being familiar with the lower court record or using oral argument to advance political or social agendas. The justices recognize that every case has a winning side and a losing side, and they accord respect to lawyers doing their best on either side.

It can also be hazardous to predict how the Court will decide a case based solely on the tenor of oral argument. After all, the justices do play devil's advocate. Years ago, I had a discussion with a justice who had a reputation for mercilessly ripping up lawyers during oral argument only to resurrect every point when writing the Court's majority opinion months later. "Why do you do that?" I asked. "He's there before his peers, his entire family, sometimes the guy's mother and father—his kids." The justice rubbed his forehead, scratched his head, and then took me quite by surprise: "You know how boring some of these cases get?"

It was now Richard Barrett's turn. It would not be boring.

> Mr. Chief Justice, if it please the Court. If the right of the people to peacefully assemble to petition the government becomes only a privilege, then the county becomes a kingdom. The courthouse is a castle, and the citizen is a subject. The moat around this castle, if you will, is the thousand-dollar permit fee for those seeking to assemble on the steps, and there is no drawbridge for either the poor who have no fee to pay for the steps or for the free who refuse to kneel upon the steps.

Barrett spoke in a clear booming voice. What was a lectern for those who had gone before was now a pulpit for him, and he would not be denied the opportunity to preach before this unusually impressive congregation.

> Here then is the battering ram against the palace of privilege: It is the inalienable and universal rights of man, and here is the crossbow against the ramparts of tyranny: It is the First Amendment. And here are the keys to the king-

dom: 1943, *Murdock*. There can be no charge for the enjoyment of a right guaranteed by the federal Constitution. 1944, *Follett.*[12] There may not even be a one-dollar per day fee to exercise rights under the First Amendment.

Chief Justice Rehnquist sought to bring Barrett closer to Earth.

CHIEF JUSTICE REHNQUIST: Mr. Barrett, do you think those cases overruled *Cox?*

MR. BARRETT: *Cox* was adopted, your Honor, at a time—

CHIEF JUSTICE REHNQUIST: Will you answer my question?

MR. BARRETT: They were consistent with *Cox*, Your Honor.

CHIEF JUSTICE REHNQUIST: But *Cox* spoke of a fee ranging from a nominal amount to three hundred dollars in 1941 and said there was nothing unconstitutional about that fee.

Barrett had dug himself a hole, but he had not yet fallen in. In fact, at times, he demonstrated a facility with the leading First Amendment precedents. One of those cases involved the principle that a speaker may not be denied a forum solely because what he has to say might be sufficiently offensive as to anger others—the so-called heckler's veto. In *Terminiello v. Chicago* (1949), the Supreme Court rejected a regulation punishing speech that "stirs the public to anger or invites dispute."[13] Barrett now turned to this case.

MR. BARRETT: Under *Terminiello,* in 1949, which is the classic case of the heckler's veto, because the cost then would be if the demonstrator says—

CHIEF JUSTICE REHNQUIST: I am not at all sure *Terminiello* is even good law anymore.

MR. BARRETT: —I am sorry, Your Honor?

CHIEF JUSTICE REHNQUIST: I said, I am not at all sure *Terminiello* is even good law anymore.

---

12. 321 U.S. 573 (1944).

13. 337 U.S. 1.

MR. BARRETT: Perhaps I can tell you how in Forsyth County, when demonstrators threatened, and also in Atlanta, which is cited somewhat in the appendix, when demonstrators said they were going to come and throw rocks and throw bricks, then the police had to respond to that emergency, and then under the county's argument, the would-be assemblers or paraders, as the case may be, are then to be charged for the cost of defending against the hecklers? I submit, Your Honor, that that simply is a heckler's veto. It is as onerous today as it is in 1949.

But when Barrett tried to argue that the Forsyth County fee disproportionately affected the poor, he got into trouble. Justice Kennedy returned to a theme pressed earlier by Justice O'Connor.

JUSTICE KENNEDY: I am not sure of the theory of your case. Suppose that an individual or a group that wanted to use the public square could afford the fee. Could the municipality charge that fee, consistent with the Constitution?

MR. BARRETT: No, Your Honor.

JUSTICE KENNEDY: Well, then, [Barrett's argument] has nothing to do with the poor.

MR. BARRETT: Nothing to do with which?

JUSTICE KENNEDY: Then it has nothing to do with the distinction in rich and poor.

MR. BARRETT: I would agree with that, Your Honor.

JUSTICE KENNEDY: So, then, we shouldn't be talking about the poor, and that was the whole thrust of your argument as I understood it.

Barrett did not appear to get the message.

MR. BARRETT: We are talking about the poor because we have a group of individuals who were denied under—

JUSTICE KENNEDY: But if the principle of the case that you are arguing has nothing to do with that, then why don't we proceed to the principle that you are arguing, and I would like to know what that principle is.

Barrett would not let go.

MR. BARRETT: Let's say for a moment that you see—here is the courthouse green. The question is, someone comes up, a veteran from another state. He says, "I want to march today" or "I want to assemble." [The county administrator] says, "Well, you didn't fill out an affidavit of poverty." What about *his* rights to travel, Your Honor? Let's say then that someone comes up and they say, "I don't want my name to be known. I don't want to sign an affidavit of poverty under the privacy provisions of the Constitution." He can't assemble then. What about someone that comes up and says, all right, I want to sign—

CHIEF JUSTICE REHNQUIST: Whoa—what are the privacy provisions of the Constitution?

One of the enduring hallmarks of Rehnquist's judicial philosophy is that the Constitution contains no right to privacy whatsoever, regardless of how valuable privacy may be to all. Rehnquist was one of the two dissenters in *Roe v. Wade* (1973),[14] the landmark decision legalizing abortion. Barrett was now in that hole.

JUSTICE KENNEDY: Counsel, you have thirty minutes. You can use the time any way you want, I suppose; we still haven't gotten to your theory of the case.

Barrett was on the ropes. He said the thousand-dollar fee limit would not save the statute because under the ordinance, the county could also impose additional charges for medical services and portable toilets. His arms flailing, his voice rising, Barrett continued.

MR. BARRETT: Since the county has already said in its brief that they regard this speech as deficient and they say that the only reason for the permit fee in their brief is to rid the public forum of unwelcome harassment, well, then, this speech must be so nauseating that they would have to charge for more toilets for the public that is going to vomit at the assembly that is wanting to be put on.

14. 410 U.S. 113.

CHIEF JUSTICE REHNQUIST: Mr. Barrett, I think you better calm down a little and address the issues. I think we have heard enough rhetoric.

MR. BARRETT: It's an emotional issue based on humanity, Your Honor.

CHIEF JUSTICE REHNQUIST: I suggest you try to keep your emotions under control and try to discuss the merits of the case.

MR. BARRETT: Certainly, Your Honor.

The white light came on at the lectern. Barrett's time was running out. He returned to the prepared script.

MR. BARRETT: I simply call the Court's attention in what meager abilities I have to Forsyth County, or any county, and ask, "What do we see here when this assembly takes place?" and "How valuable is that to America?" I see Americana and I see the stump speech. I can't put a price on it, but I see the furrowed brow of labor listening. I see the tender graces of motherhood feeling. I hear the assertion of youth speaking out—

JUSTICE SCALIA: I see the mother paying out in municipal taxes what she might be buying food for her child with. *[laughter]*

MR. BARRETT: Balance that if you will, Your Honor, between perhaps the sharpening right there of democracy's rusty instruments. Can I speak of the spoken word and the sparks that come from it? Can I speak of reason and the glitter that lightens our minds? Can I speak of the shiny sword of reason that ousts tyranny from among us? Your Honor, they have spoken of money. May I speak of freedom? They have spoken of convenience. May I speak of happiness? Someone asked if I would pay a fee. Your Honor, write this epitaph, if you will, on my tomb: "The road not taken, but not the speech not given."

CHIEF JUSTICE REHNQUIST: How about the argument not made!

The only justice not to speak was Clarence Thomas. He rarely asks any questions during oral argument, and from time to time goes years without a single inquiry. The only explanation from chambers is that Thomas believes his colleagues take up too much of the lawyers' time.

In this case, it helped prevent what could have developed into an unseemly confrontation. Court sources, speaking on the condition of anonymity, have confirmed the U.S. Marshals Service had dispatched additional security to the courtroom for Barrett's presentation—not knowing what to expect but not wanting to take any chances.

In the pressroom following the hearing, the talk was how Barrett had self-destructed during the argument. I kept my own counsel. Based on all that he had told me the night before and what I had learned subsequently, I thought Barrett had done rather well—it could have been significantly worse.

The Court's decision in a case isn't usually announced until weeks, often months, after the case is argued. For example, the landmark affirmative action case, *Regents University of California v. Alan Bakke,* was argued on October 12, 1977, but the decision wasn't announced until June 28, 1978.[15] According to well-placed sources, Justice Lewis F. Powell Jr.'s controlling opinion was completed by Thanksgiving. The remaining eight justices needed seven months fully to articulate what they thought of the case (and offer their own spins on what their colleagues were writing).

But cases argued on Monday (such as the Forsyth County case) and Tuesday come up for a vote immediately at the justices' regular Wednesday afternoon conference. Cases argued on Wednesday are voted on at the justices' Friday conferences. Rarely—maybe once or twice a year—do these tentative votes ever change. And so it was in the case of *Forsyth County, Georgia v. the Nationalist Movement.*

The justices gathered in their conference room on April 2. This is a highly confidential meeting—no secretaries, no law clerks, only the nine justices. The junior justice, at this time Clarence Thomas, acts as the official notetaker. While there is no formal record of the meeting, time-honored procedures provide some glimpses and hints about how the case probably went down. The chief justice sits at the head of a long, rectangular table and speaks first. The chief may briefly outline the issue

15. 438 U.S. 265 (1978).

in the case as he sees it before declaring his view of how the case should be decided. Chief Justice Rehnquist was not in Barrett's corner. The chief explained that he was persuaded that *Cox v. New Hampshire* was controlling—just as the Forsyth County attorney had argued—and that *Cox* remained good law and should not be overruled.

There is very little debate in these conferences. In speeches, Rehnquist has explained that the case is considered twice, "once with [the lawyers] and once without." That, however, is largely incorrect. The oral argument is the only occasion where all the justices discuss the case together at any length—one of the features that makes oral argument so important. Nearly all the other communication among the justices regarding pending cases is in writing and is distributed to all. The chief had spoken. Justice Stevens—the senior justice, sitting at the opposite end of the table—was next. Stevens saw a clear First Amendment violation in the Forsyth County fee arrangement, disagreeing with the chief. The vote continued by seniority, with Thomas recording the votes and knowing that as junior justice, he would vote last. Were his colleagues to split four-to-four, his vote would be decisive. Byron R. "Whizzer" White was next, agreeing with Rehnquist. Justice Harry A. Blackmun agreed with Stevens, as did O'Connor. Then came Justice Scalia, who throughout the argument had faulted the Movement's CEO-lawyer for not making his case. Despite his apparent apprehensions about the discretion given the county administrator to set the fee, Scalia voted to reverse, siding with the county. The score was 3-3, with three justices yet to vote. Justice Kennedy: affirm. Justice Souter: affirm. And that was it. Souter had provided the crucial fifth vote to affirm. Richard Barrett and his white supremacist movement had won the case. Thomas voted to reverse. Stevens, the senior justice on the winning side, got to assign who would write the opinion for the Court. He gave it to Blackmun, who announced the 5-4 decision on June 19, 1992, eighty days after the case had been argued.

Blackmun's opinion for the Court follows closely the concerns expressed during the oral argument by Justice Scalia (whose vote he failed to pick up) and Justice Souter's concern that the fee could operate as a heckler's veto. The problem for the Court was that the county administrator had "unbridled discretion" to determine how much to charge for police protection or administrative time—or even whether to charge at all. The administrator was not required to rely on any objective standards or to provide any explanation for his or her decision. The majority was also troubled that to accurately assess the cost of security for parade participants, the administrator must evaluate the message conveyed and estimate the public response to that message.

In his dissenting opinion (joined by White, Scalia, and Thomas), Rehnquist wrote that the Court's analysis was based "on an assumption that the county will interpret the phrase 'maintenance of public order' to support the imposition of fees based on opposition crowds. There is nothing in the record to support this assumption, however, and I would remand for a hearing on this question." Rehnquist also concluded that the Constitution "does not limit a parade license fee to a nominal amount," an issue the Court's majority avoided.[16]

It was Richard Barrett's first and only appearance in the U.S. Supreme Court, an important First Amendment case in which he can claim victory. Not having returned, he also has a claim that none of the truly great advocates in Supreme Court history can make—he's undefeated. A perfect record, albeit for a less-than-perfect performance.

Barrett has gone on to fight new battles on behalf of his Nationalist Movement. In 2005, he tried to organize an "Edgar Ray Killen Appreciation Day," honoring the Ku Klux Klansman convicted of instigating the murder of three civil rights workers in Mississippi in 1964, infamous murders that formed the basis for the 1988 movie *Mississippi Burning*. Prior to Killen's conviction, Barrett also touched off a furor by attempting to set up a booth at the Mississippi State Fair at which Killen would sign autographs and solicit contributions for his defense. Barrett abandoned the idea when Killen advised that he would be unable to attend.

And while Barrett has not been back to the U.S. Supreme Court, his mission has made him a frequent visitor in the lower courts. When Morristown, New Jersey, sought to require Barrett to show proof of insurance before allowing him to hold a Fourth of July rally in 2001, Bar-

16. 505 U.S. 140 (1992).

rett went to court, again alleging a First Amendment violation. The court agreed. The rally did not amount to much, attracting fewer than a dozen participants. The Nationalist Movement still profited handsomely from the event, with Barrett collecting an estimated thirty thousand dollars in legal fees on behalf of his organization—not bad for an outfit that ten years earlier had less than a hundred dollars in assets. If nothing else, Barrett and his case provide powerful evidence that the First Amendment remains alive and well.

Forsyth County v. the Nationalist Movement and the other cases described in this book are, of course, only a small chapter in the life of the U.S. Supreme Court. But even these cases show how great a role the high court plays in the everyday lives of all Americans, a role that is magnified over time. Veteran journalist Morton Mintz, who for many years covered the Supreme Court for the *Washington Post,* has observed that there is probably no greater barometer of what is on the minds of the U.S. population than the docket of the U.S. Supreme Court. I concur. All Americans should have the same front-row seat, via their television sets, that my colleagues and I have enjoyed for so many years. Such seats are available in most courtrooms, as many states allow television coverage of their trials and appellate hearings, which are rarely momentous, with no noticeable adverse effects.

As Charles Bierbauer explains in his analysis of *Bush v. Gore* in this book, the Supreme Court will not allow television coverage of its arguments in even the most momentous cases. In the Supreme Court, the principal arguments against cameras in court—that witnesses or jurors might be intimidated—do not apply. There are no witnesses or jurors to be intimidated. And the arguments in favor of televised court coverage generally would seem to apply with special force in the U.S. Supreme Court. Not only are the cases of interest to many Americans, but many Americans are directly affected by what the high court decides.

The justices' primary concern appears to be that television might give a distorted view of how the Court operates in that arguments would be edited for the evening news. This is inevitably correct. Complex issues would be reduced to simplified sound bites and narration. It does not necessarily follow, however, that the distortion that editing creates would in any way harm the Court or that the editing would differ in any meaningful way from that in the print media.

Justice Souter is apparently concerned that he personally might be intimidated by the cameras—that based on his experience as a justice on the New Hampshire Supreme Court, he might not want to ask questions for fear of how his questions might be presented on the evening news. Appearing before the House Appropriations Committee on March 28, 1996, Souter stated that "the case [against televised coverage] is so strong that I can tell you the day you see a camera come into our courtroom, it's going to roll over my dead body." One would hate to see it come to that. Souter is genuinely well liked, especially by his peers on the Court. His fear appears to be that by playing devil's advocate, as Supreme Court justices frequently do, the advocate part might be lost on the evening news.

These fears are misplaced. Like the disadvantages, the benefits of showing Supreme Court arguments on the evening news have been quite exaggerated. The real benefit has nothing to do with the news media per se. The real plus is that cable channels—such as C-SPAN and perhaps others—would be permitted to broadcast the hearings in their entirety, with no distortion or editing whatsoever. Although hardly the stuff of commercial prime time, gavel-to-gavel coverage would be invaluable to lawyers, law students, judges, and countless other Americans who care deeply not only about the issues on which the Court decides but also about the Court itself.

A few years ago, I asked one of the Court's leading opponents of televised coverage if he would still object to television coverage if only C-SPAN broadcast the hearings and the arguments were not made available to the commercial TV news media. "That would be okay," was this justice's reply, "but we couldn't do that. There is no way." Well, maybe not as a matter of constitutional law. But, as a practical matter, the justices *could* quite easily do it. Justice Scalia, among those on the Court known to oppose televised coverage, may have stumbled onto the answer in a televised interview with Tim Russert of NBC News that appeared on C-SPAN in 2005. Scalia correctly observed that the news media have a notoriously short attention span: "*Bush v. Gore,* or any other case, is of immense importance to the press the day the argument is held," said Scalia, "but if the tape is released the next day, phew!—it's used for wrapping fish" (2005). In recognition of that failing, the Court could release videotapes two or three days after a case is argued. While the TV media, in Scalia's words, might wrap their fish in it, C-SPAN could (and I'm told *would*) show many of the arguments to those who care on its regular Saturday program, *America and the Courts*. Percentage-wise, it would be a small audience. But even if only one in a hundred Americans would watch, that would still add up to nearly three hundred thousand viewers whose interest in the Court and its work should not be lightly dismissed. This compromise is based on the concerns of Justice Souter and some of his colleagues that oral argument would be portrayed on the evening news in a context that harms either the justices themselves or the Court as an institution, a concern I emphatically do not share. At minimum, the matter should be put to a majority vote of the Court; the issue is sufficiently important that neither Souter nor any other justice should be allowed to trump the will of the majority.

The Supreme Court works very well—arguably, more in keeping with what the Framers of our Constitution had in mind than any other institution of government. Few can know or appreciate this virtue, however, because so few can actually see for themselves. The justices would better serve themselves and the country by heeding the famous advice of one of the Court's most respected members of all time, Louis D. Brandeis: "Sunlight is the best of disinfectants" (1933, 62).

Planned Parenthood of S.E. Pennsylvania v. Casey

The Rhetorical Battle over *Roe*

ARGUED APRIL 22, 1992

LYLE DENNISTON

The Pennsylvania legislature amended its abortion control law in 1988 and 1989. Among the new provisions, the law required informed consent and a twenty-four-hour waiting period prior to the procedure. A minor seeking an abortion required the consent of one parent, although the law included a procedure for judicial bypass. A married woman seeking an abortion had to indicate that she had notified her husband of her intention to abort the fetus. Several abortion clinics and physicians, including Planned Parenthood of Southeastern Pennsylvania, challenged these provisions. A federal appeals court upheld all the provisions except for the requirement that husbands be notified.

To listen to passages from oral arguments indicated with 🔊, visit www.goodquarrel.com.

NOVEMBER 7, 1991, WAS A DAY OF REMEMBRANCE AND SYMBOLism for the women's rights movement in America. It was the seventy-fifth anniversary of the day that feminist Jeannette Rankin became the first woman to win election to Congress. Nadine Strossen, the president of the American Civil Liberties Union (ACLU), took note of that anniversary from the podium in the ballroom of the Washington Court Hotel in downtown Washington, D.C.

The year 1991, Strossen also remembered, was the two hundredth anniversary of the ratification of the Bill of Rights. But she and the other feminist leaders holding a press conference that day were not in a celebrating mood. Said Strossen, "If the Supreme Court overturns *Roe v. Wade,*[1] which it seems poised to do, it would be the first time in the nation's history that the U.S. Supreme Court would take away a fundamental individual constitutional right. What an ironic first to celebrate on the bicentennial of the Bill of Rights, and on Jeannette Rankin's anniversary. What a sad thing if she could see that."[2] But amid the pessimism, the four women who took turns at the microphone on that day also expressed a hardheaded determination not to surrender.

The first to speak, Kathryn Kolbert, an ACLU lawyer in Philadelphia, announced to reporters that a new appeal had just been filed at the Supreme Court in a Pennsylvania abortion case; the lawyers had put it on a fast track in hopes of getting it decided before the Court finished its 1991 term the following summer. Kolbert commented, "We have presented one question and only one question to the nine justices: Has the Supreme Court overruled *Roe v. Wade?*"

It did not sound like the kind of question one puts before the Supreme Court. As a matter of pure fact, the Supreme Court had not overruled *Roe.* A single-word answer is not the kind the Supreme Court gives. But Kolbert had not misspoken. When ACLU aides passed out copies of the petition, there it was, on the page just inside the cover.

---

1. 410 U.S. 113 (1973).

2. This quote and those that follow from the November 7, 1991, press conference are from the author's notes of the event.

QUESTION PRESENTED

1. Has the Supreme Court overruled *Roe v. Wade,* 410 U.S. 113 (1973), holding that a woman's right to choose abortion is a fundamental right protected by the United States Constitution?

There was no question 2.

"Some may argue," Kolbert conceded, "that asking that question is a risky endeavor." Indeed, Linda Greenhouse (1992) later wrote, "The strategy that the abortion-rights side brought to the Supreme Court . . . had every appearance of a high-stakes gamble." But the other speakers clearly demonstrated that they all had embraced a strategy that was bold, even risky, an outright mix of law and politics. The speakers believed that the Supreme Court would be setting the stage for the 1992 presidential and congressional elections and for state ballot battles over at least a dozen anti-abortion referenda.

Kate Michelman, then the executive director of the National Abortion Rights Action League and perhaps the most politically attuned leader on the podium, soon threw down the political gauntlet: "With the Pennsylvania case before the Court, the 1992 election becomes ever more critical. . . . One year from now, Americans go to the polls. The Pennsylvania case creates ever more urgency for the right to choose—it is a key issue, a voting issue, a winning issue." Added Faye Wattleton, the president of the Planned Parenthood Federation of America, "It is better that the decision gets made as quickly as possible. Certainly it will be a major issue in this election. . . . If politicians do not protect our rights, they will not get our votes."

Politics often is a driving force in big Supreme Court cases, but it is usually politics in the broadest sense—using the processes of government to achieve a desired social goal; *Roe v. Wade* itself was an example. Seldom do lawyers shape a lawsuit before the Court with the specific aim of influencing an election's outcome. But that was a core part of the strategy for *Planned Parenthood of Southeastern Pennsylvania v. Casey* (1992).[3] The case was docketed as no. 91-744 in the Supreme

3. 505 U.S. 833.

Court on November 7, 1991. It was then consolidated with an appeal filed on December 11, 1991, by the state of Pennsylvania. The cases were granted together on January 21, 1992, argued on April 22, and decided on June 29.

Lawyers who take cases to the Supreme Court, even in major cases, ordinarily focus primarily on the justices: whose vote is already lost to my client, whose votes can I count on, how do I get to five votes? The larger political and social community is a secondary audience, left to the blandishments of publicists and organizational spokespersons. But to Kolbert and her associates, the audiences were one and the same. Putting an electoral ambition right alongside a legal aspiration, as they were doing, had enormous potential complications. Every filing in the case would be a political document as well as a legal paper; if the Court agreed to hear the case, every word of oral argument would be a political as well as a legal statement. In oral argument, the Court does not favor political assertions unless they are quite well disguised as legal claims. The abortion rights advocates would present *Roe*'s future as a constitutional question, to be sure, but it would be a political platform, too.

Their case, of course, raised other questions not recited in their petition—the constitutionality of five features of a Pennsylvania state law: doctors had to provide an "informed consent" message to women seeking abortions, and women then had to wait twenty-four hours before obtaining abortions; parents had to consent before teenagers could have abortions; providers needed to report to the state on each abortion performed; there were limited medical emergency exceptions to the law's requirements; and women had to tell their husbands before having abortions.

The U.S. Circuit Court of Appeals for the Third Circuit, based in Philadelphia, struck down only the spousal-notice provision, upholding all of the remainder of the state statute. Judge Samuel A. Alito Jr., then in his eighteenth month of service on the circuit court, dissented from the court's ruling on the spousal-notice provision, a position that Wattleton denounced at the November 1991 press conference as the equivalent of making a woman "a reproductive chattel of her husband." Judge

Alito's vote in the case became an issue in 2006, when the Senate Judiciary Committee reviewed his nomination to the Supreme Court. For those planning the abortion rights appeal to the Supreme Court, however, those were side issues, merely illustrative of the threat if *Roe v. Wade* were to be weakened or overruled. They had their reasons for keeping the fate of *Roe* at the center of their strategy.

Just two years earlier, in the Court's 5-4 decision in a Missouri abortion case, *Webster v. Reproductive Health Services,* Justice Harry A. Blackmun, the author of *Roe* and still its fervent champion, had written, "Today, *Roe v. Wade* . . . and the fundamental constitutional right of women to decide whether to terminate a pregnancy, survive but are not secure. . . . I fear for the future. I fear for the liberty and equality of the millions of women who have lived and come of age in the 16 years since *Roe* was decided. I fear for the integrity of, and public esteem for, this Court. . . . For today, at least, the law of abortion stands undisturbed. For today, the women of this Nation still retain the liberty to control their destinies. But the signs are evident and very ominous and a chill wind blows."[4]

And in an opinion concurring in part in the judgment, Justice Sandra Day O'Connor said, "[T]here is no necessity to accept the State's invitation to reexamine the constitutional validity of *Roe v. Wade*. . . . When the constitutional invalidity of a State's abortion statute actually turns on the constitutional validity of *Roe v. Wade,* there will be time enough to reexamine *Roe*. And to do so carefully."[5]

Two years after *Webster,* the Court had changed markedly, leading to the pessimism in the abortion rights community. Justices William J. Brennan Jr. and Thurgood Marshall, two close allies of Blackmun on abortion rights, had been replaced by Justice David H. Souter, presumed—at least by women's rights groups—to be a foe of *Roe,* and Justice Clarence Thomas, a conservative assumed to be a sure vote against *Roe*'s continuing validity. In fact, feminist organizations had strenuously opposed Souter's nomination. In late September 1990, after Souter

4. 492 U.S. 490 (1989), at 537, 538, 559.

5. 492 U.S. 522, 525–26.

had appeared before the Senate Judiciary Committee, the National Organization for Women had staged a "Do or Die Day" lobbying rally in downtown Washington, announced by bright red posters blaring "Stop Souter or Women Will Die" (Denniston 1990). The opposition to Thomas was even more vehement. The votes, it seemed, were there to strike down *Roe*.

But when the Court announced on January 21 that it would hear *Casey* and the state's companion appeal, the justices sent the clearest possible signal that they were not ready to assist Kolbert in her sweeping legal/political challenge. The order granting review (which Justice Souter had drafted, with editing by Justice John Paul Stevens) read, in part, "The petitions for writ of certiorari are granted limited to the following questions: 1. Did the Court of Appeals err in upholding the constitutionality of . . . provisions of the Pennsylvania Abortion Control Act? . . . 2. Did the Court of Appeals err in holding [spousal notice] unconstitutional?"[6]

To lawyers appearing regularly before the Court, the phrase *limited to* was close to a firm mandate. This time, though, it was not much of a limitation. The federal government, speaking through the U.S. solicitor general, had once again urged the Court to overrule *Roe* (Denniston 1992), "as it had done in five other cases in the last decade," the Court noted in its ultimate ruling.[7] And Kolbert and her legal team continued to maintain that the Pennsylvania case was primarily about *Roe*. Their brief on the merits made a bow to the Court's rewriting of the questions at issue; it simply recited them as the Court had done in its order. But the merits brief devoted the first twenty-six pages of a forty-eight-page argument section to the plea to reaffirm *Roe* and the right to choose as "a fundamental right protected," by the Constitution (Kolbert et al. 1992, 41).

On April 22, the Court inexplicably opened its argument session two minutes early according to the clock above the bench. Kolbert was ready. Her task was formidable: as Chief Justice William H. Rehnquist

6. 502 U.S. 1056 (1992).

7. 505 U.S. 844.

called the case, the lawyer looked up at a bench with only two seemingly supportive justices, Blackmun and Stevens. She would have to persuade three other justices to prevail on any point. But that was the long shot part of her strategy; a self-confident advocate, she had planned to make the next hour about *Roe.* And at that moment, Kolbert—seasoned as a lawyer, a novice as a political operative—also sought to launch the most visible part of the women's rights movement's 1992 election campaign.

> Mr. Chief Justice and may it please the Court: Whether our Constitution endows government with the power to force a woman to continue or to end a pregnancy against her will is the central question in this case. Since this Court's decision in *Roe v. Wade,* a generation of American women has come of age secure in the knowledge that the Constitution provides the highest level of protection for their child-bearing decisions.
>
> The genius of *Roe* and the Constitution is that it fully protects rights of fundamental importance. Government may not chip away at fundamental rights, nor make them selectively available only to the most privileged women.

For eight minutes, an unusual span for the Court to sit silently, merely listening, the Court allowed Kolbert to proceed uninterrupted without discussing the questions the Court's order had posed. Spectators in the courtroom noticed that except for Justices O'Connor and Souter, the Court's members were not looking at Kolbert, instead keeping their eyes on briefs stacked in front of them. The only sounds in the courtroom were Kolbert's voice—unhurried, nearly free of passion, unaccented except for a flattening of some of her *A*s—and the barely heard rustle as she turned the pages of her prepared notes.

Finally, Justice O'Connor spoke up: "Ms. Kolbert, um, you're arguing the case as though all we have before us is whether to apply stare decisis and preserve *Roe* against *Wade* in all its aspects. Nevertheless, we granted certiorari on some specific questions in this case. Do you plan to address any of those in your argument?" As was often true when she thought lawyers were straying, O'Connor, though speaking quietly, sounded perplexed, a bit put off.

"Your Honor, I do," Kolbert answered. "However, the central question in this case is what is the standard that this Court used to evaluate the restrictions that are at issue, and therefore one cannot—" O'Connor interrupted: "Well, the standard may affect the outcome or it may not, but at bottom we still have to deal with specific issues, and I wondered if you were going to address them?" Kolbert responded, "Yes, I am, Your Honor, and I would like in particular to address the husband-notification provisions, but the standard that this Court applies will well establish the outcome in this case for a variety of reasons." If she was intending to get to the Pennsylvania statute, she was not doing so. It was by now abundantly clear that she would not be diverted from her chosen mission, to put the Court to the test on *Roe*. She and her colleagues had not spent months strategizing only to change course now. However insistent the Court might be on keeping the *Casey* case within narrow bounds, the constitutional and political agendas on Kolbert's side required her to hold steady.

After O'Connor failed to pull Kolbert back to the Pennsylvania statute, Justice Antonin G. Scalia toyed with her a bit about what historical frames of reference the Court should use in judging whether abortion rights could be read into the Constitution; he had no intention of voting for her, but no one else was interrupting her, and Scalia was not inclined just to hear her out.

JUSTICE SCALIA: Ms Kolbert, on this last point, I am not sure what you suggest we look to. You say we should not look to what the practice was in 1868. Should we look to what the practice was at the time of *Roe,* or what the practice is today—that is, what the states would do, left to their own devices?

MS. KOLBERT: Your Honor, I believe that you have to look very generally at whether the nation's history and tradition has respected interests of bodily integrity and autonomy and whether there has been a tradition of respect for equality of women. Those are the central and core values—

JUSTICE SCALIA: But not to abortion in particular?

MS. KOLBERT: Well, this Court is—if the Court was only to look at whether abortion was illegal in 1868—that is, at the time of the adoption of the Fourteenth Amendment—it would be placed in a very difficult situation because at the time of the founding of the nation, at the time that the Constitution was adopted, abortion was legal.

JUSTICE SCALIA: Well, pick 1968; I gather you wouldn't accept 1968 either, though.

MS. KOLBERT: Well, we think that the Court ought to look generally at the principles that this decision protects. That while it is important to look—and I would not urge you to ignore the state of the law at different periods of our history, it is only one factor in a variety of factors that this Court has to look to in determining whether or not something is fundamental. And fundamental status in this instance derives from a history of this Court's acknowledgment and acceptance that private, autonomous decisions made by women in the privacy of their families ought to be respected and accorded fundamental status. Certainly, the anomalous posture of the fact that abortion was legal at the time of the founding of the Constitution and then illegal at the time of the adoption of the Fourteenth Amendment would place this Court in a very difficult position—that is, rights may be guaranteed under the Fifth Amendment and not the Fourteenth merely because only the exact state of the law in 1868 is the factor that the Court accepts.

JUSTICE SCALIA: This is not an antiquarian argument you are making. I mean, you would have made the same argument in 1868. I think you would have said the mere fact that most states disfavor abortion is no justification for this Court's saying that it is not therefore included within it. You would have made that same argument in 1868.

MS. KOLBERT: I would, and that is the argument that this Court has made in many instances in rejecting exactly the state of the law prior to the granting of fundamental status. That is, this Court, if we were only to look at whether state legislatures prohibited activity in determining whether or not an activity is fundamental, many of the most precious rights that we now have—rights to travel, rights to vote, rights to be free from racial segregation—would not be accorded status because in fact, state legislators have acted to inhibit those rights at the time of the adoption of the Fourteenth Amendment.

JUSTICE SCALIA: Some of those are mentioned in the Constitution, like racial segregation.

MS. KOLBERT: Your Honor, this Court has recognized that the rights at issue here—that is, the rights of privacy, the rights of autonomy—flow from the liberty clause of the Fourteenth Amendment, which is also mentioned in the Constitution. The debate centers on what is the meaning of that term, *liberty,* and we think that the precedents of this Court that began at the end of the nineteenth century and have proceeded from this Court to the very present, would logically and necessarily include fundamental rights to decide whether to carry a pregnancy to term or to terminate that pregnancy.

Kolbert was past the halfway mark of her thirty minutes at the lectern. Justice Anthony M. Kennedy, showing some impatience, told her, "I don't question the importance of your arguing that there is a fundamental right, as you have done. . . . But one way of our understanding this fundamental rights and their parameters, their dimensions, is to decide on a case-by-case basis, and you have a number of specific provisions here that I think you should address."

She began an answer, again focusing on "the standard of *Roe,*" but Kennedy shortly cut her off. "I am suggesting," he said, "that our sustaining these statutory provisions does not necessarily undercut all of the holding of *Roe v. Wade.*" She was not sensitive to the nudge: "To adopt a lesser standard . . . would be the same as overruling *Roe.*" "Well," Kennedy retorted, "if you are going to argue that *Roe* can survive only in its most rigid formulation, that is an election you can make as counsel. I am suggesting to you that that is not the only logical possibility in this case."

Kolbert drew O'Connor into a brief exchange about what *Roe* had actually held as a matter of law and then used that discussion as a predicate for new emphasis on her reading of *Roe.*

MS. KOLBERT: Our position is that *Roe,* in establishing a trimester framework, in establishing strict scrutiny, and in also establishing that the rights of women and the health interests of women always take precedent over the state's interest in potential life. Those hallmarks of *Roe* are central to this case and are central to continuing recognition of the right as fundamental. Should the Court abandon that—

JUSTICE O'CONNOR: But did the Court hold that, even after viability of the fetus in *Roe?*

MS. KOLBERT: What the Court—

JUSTICE O'CONNOR: Do you think that was a correct characterization of *Roe*'s holding that you just gave, that the woman's interest always takes precedence? Is that true under *Roe,* in the latter stages of pregnancy?

MS. KOLBERT: Your Honor, under *Roe,* after the point of viability, that is the point when the fetus is capable of survival, the state is free to prohibit abortion but only so long as it is necessary, only so long as the woman's health interests and life interests are not at stake. That is, potential fetal life is a recognized value, is a recognized state interest after the point of viability, but when in conflict, when the woman's health interest is in conflict with those state interests and potential life, those women's interest, the women's interest in health takes precedent. Now, admittedly, the question of viability and the viability line is not as present in this case as it has been in many of the other cases that this Court has seen before here. That is, all of the restrictions that are at issue in Pennsylvania attach in pregnancy at the very beginning of pregnancy, and therefore the state's interest in protection of fetal life really does not come into play. The real issue is whether or not these health interests—that is, whether or not the state's interest in protecting a compelling interest in health are present.

And frankly, this Court need only look to the record—that is, need only look to the findings of the district court—to determine that this statute in no way furthers women's health interests.

Finally, with but moments left in her argument time, she began discussing her objections to the particular provisions of the Pennsylvania law; no parts of the law, she said, were reasonable. "The extensive record here," she said, "demonstrates that the harms are not speculative nor remote, nor is this a worst-case scenario. . . . Pennsylvania women should not be the guinea pigs in the state's experiment with constitutional law." Her final target was the provision requiring the husband's notification. Before sitting down, she offered the Court a concluding bit of oratory: "In the days before *Roe,* thousands of women lost their lives and more were subjected to physical and emotional scars from back-alley and self-induced abortions. Recognizing that, this Court established *Roe* and established fundamental protection for women's childbearing decisions. We urge this Court to reaffirm those principles today."

Pennsylvania's attorney general, Ernest D. Preate Jr., opened with a suggestion that "*Roe v. Wade* need not be revisited by this Court except to reaffirm that *Roe* did not establish an absolute right to abortion on demand but rather a limited right subject to reasonable state regulations designed to serve important and legitimate state—" Blackmun cut off the end of Preate's sentence, the only comment or question the justice uttered. He tartly reminded Preate that *Roe* "does not provide for abortion on demand"—though Preate had not said that it did. Condescendingly, Blackmun asked, "Have you read *Roe?*" It was a startling question, provoking an audible gasp in the courtroom. Preate said he had read it, and Blackmun said simply, "Thank you."

Because Preate was eager to discuss the specifics of the Pennsylvania law and downplay the state's backup argument that *Roe* should be overruled if the state law would fall under a less restrictive constitutional standard, several justices engaged him on the rationale behind the restrictions. The argument did not go well for Preate or for the state statute. His argument lost its crispness, and he stopped finishing some of his sentences. He spent nearly all of his time defending the spousal-notice provision. The exchanges primarily revealed considerable skepticism from Justices O'Connor, Stevens, and Kennedy.

JUSTICE O'CONNOR: Now, the provision does not require notification to a father who is not the husband, I take it.

MR. PREATE: That's correct, Justice O'Connor, . . . or notice if the woman is unmarried. It only applies to married women.

JUSTICE O'CONNOR: So what's the interest, to try to preserve the marriage?

MR. PREATE: There are several good interests—the interest, of course, in protecting the life of the unborn child.

JUSTICE O'CONNOR: Well, then, why not require notice to all fathers? It's a curious sort of a provision, isn't it?

MR. PREATE: It is that, but the legislature has made the judgment that it wanted its statute to apply in this specific instance because it wanted to further the integrity of marriages.

JUSTICE O'CONNOR: Would you say that the state could similarly require a woman to notify anyone with whom she had intercourse that she planned to use some means of birth control after the intercourse that operates, let's say, as an abortifacient? Could the state do that? I mean, it would be the same state interest, I suppose.

MR. PREATE: The state interest would be the same, but I think that would be problematic. I'm not—

JUSTICE O'CONNOR: And why would it be problematic, do you think?

MR. PREATE: I think that with regard to applying a statute to all women, that it might create a severe obstacle, an absolute obstacle to their obtaining an abortion.

JUSTICE O'CONNOR: I don't understand.

MR. PREATE: The undue-burden standard, as I understand it, is that whether or not the regulation would impose such an absolute obstacle, not whether it would deter or inhibit some women from obtaining an abortion.

JUSTICE O'CONNOR: Well, we're talking about the provision for notification in this case under the statute to the husband, and I'm just asking whether a different type of state regulation would have to be upheld under your standard.

Justice Stevens also pressed for answers about the restrictions.

JUSTICE STEVENS: No, but General, may I ask you a question. Is it not true, therefore, that the only people affected by the statute, this very small group, are people who would not otherwise notify their husbands?

MR. PREATE: I'm not sure I got all of that question, Justice Stevens.

JUSTICE STEVENS: Well, you've demonstrated that the public interest is in a very limited group of people, the few women who would not otherwise notify their husbands, and those are the only people affected by the statute.

MR. PREATE: That is correct.

JUSTICE STEVENS: Everyone in that class, should we not assume, would not notify her husband but for the statute?

MR. PREATE: That is correct. In that 1 percent, not everyone would want to notify, and there are exceptions.

JUSTICE STEVENS: They would not [notify] without the statute.

MR. PREATE: They would not [notify] without the statute, but there are exceptions, several of them—four.

JUSTICE STEVENS: No, they'd only—you've already taken the exceptions into account in narrowing the group very—to, you know, 1 percent, or whatever it is.

MR. PREATE: Justice—

JUSTICE STEVENS: You aren't suggesting there's no one whose decision will be affected by the statute?

MR. PREATE: Well, that's the point. On this record, which is what we have to go on, there is nothing established by the petitioners as to how many there are in that category.

JUSTICE STEVENS: Well, if there's no one affected by the statute, what is the state interest in upholding the statute?

MR. PREATE: The state interest in upholding the statute is the protection of the life of the unborn and the protection of the marital integrity and to ensuring of communication, the possibility—we are not asking—

Justice Kennedy then expressed his confusion regarding the spousal notification requirement.

JUSTICE KENNEDY: It's a very strange argument to say that the law doesn't affect 90 percent of the people so we're not concerned with the law. I've never heard that argument.

Justice Souter also inquired briefly about this requirement. His attempt to draw out Preate was cut short by the end of the attorney general's time.

JUSTICE SOUTER: Mister Preate, because you have a little time left, there is one point on which I guess I never fully followed your argument, and I wonder if you would go back to it. You got to the point, you were arguing about the number of instances, the percentage of instances in which the spousal notification would in fact make a difference in the behavior of the parties involved. And as I recall, you got it down to about 5 percent to begin with who would not otherwise, 5 percent of the women who would not otherwise give notice to their spouses. Then from that 5 percent you subtracted some number for those, I guess subject to medical emergencies, those subject to the certification that they would be physically abused, and I think by that process of elimination you got it down to about 1 percent who would actually be affected by the stricture of the statute, is that right?

MR. PREATE: That is not correct, Justice—you start with the 1 percent because 95 percent of 20 percent is 1 percent. You are talking about five hundred women that—

JUSTICE SOUTER: You are talking about all women, but the spousal notification applies only to married women.

MR. PREATE: That is correct.

JUSTICE SOUTER: What is the percentage of married women? Well, your time is up.

MR. PREATE: Sorry.

Scalia had attempted, without notable success, to rehabilitate Preate's argument by pointing out the problem with the undue-burden standard.

JUSTICE SCALIA: General Preate, I thought we were talking not rational basis but undue burden. Are they the same thing?

MR. PREATE: No, they are not, Justice Scalia.

JUSTICE SCALIA: How do I go about determining whether it's an undue burden or not? What law books do I look to?

Representing the administration of President George H. W. Bush, solicitor general Kenneth W. Starr, whose brief had recommended that *Roe* be cast aside, chose to focus on a plea to adopt a more tolerant test for judging restrictions on abortions. A smooth and practiced advocate, he talked at length before being pressed, somewhat brusquely, by Justice Byron R. White to state exactly what standard he advocated.

JUSTICE WHITE: What is the standard? And you started out to tell us what the standard was?

MR. STARR: We believe it was articulated, Justice White, by the *Webster* plurality.

JUSTICE WHITE: Well, what is it?

MR. STARR: It is the rational-basis standard. And that is the standard that has been articulated by this Court in a variety of decisions and by a variety of justices of this Court, in its abortion jurisprudence.[8]

JUSTICE WHITE: And under that standard, you would think all of the provisions that are at issue here should be sustained?

MR. STARR: Exactly.

Justice Souter sought to find out "where the standard would take us," wondering if it would permit complete prohibition of abortions. Starr said that "very serious questions" would arise if the standard went that far, but he conceded that "the rational-basis standard would, in fact, allow considerable leeway to the states, if it saw fit."

Justice Stevens, leaving no doubt about how he would vote, questioned Starr about the government's view that states had an interest in the life of fetuses throughout pregnancy, an interest that would practi-

8. Although it was never advocated by a majority of justices.

cally, if not absolutely, allow a total ban on abortions. Stevens joined Souter in critiquing Starr's proposed standard. The argument had moved to terrain that was inhospitable to Starr's argument, and his presentation lost some of its finesse.

JUSTICE STEVENS: That's not really a fair answer. Rational basis under your analysis: there's an interest in preserving fetal life at all times during pregnancy. It's rational, under your view. Ergo it follows that a total prohibition, protected by criminal penalties, would be rational, it would meet your standard.

MR. STARR: I don't think so. The common law, the common—

JUSTICE STEVENS: Well—what is your rational-basis standard if not the traditional one?

MR. STARR: Ours is the traditional one. But under that traditional analysis, there must, in fact, be a rational connection with a legitimate state interest, and the state cannot proceed in an arbitrary and capricious fashion, in my view. If I may complete this, I think this is an important part of the answer. It would be arbitrary and capricious. It would, moreover, deprive an individual of her right to life if there were not an emergency exception. And even in *Roe v. Wade*, the Texas statute at issue there provided for that exception. It would be quite at war with our traditions, as embodied in the common law, not to provide, at a minimum, for that kind of exception.

JUSTICE STEVENS: No, but what you're saying is the rational-basis standard, which normally just requires a reason that is legitimate to support it, can be overcome in some cases by countervailing interest, which is not the normal rational-basis standard.

MR. STARR: Well, may I respond? . . . I think that the traditional rational-basis test does, in fact, analyze the ends. It looks at the ends and the means. And it requires, in fact, that the state not conduct itself in an arbitrary and capricious fashion. That is the ultimate insight of the rational-basis test.

Kolbert, with three minutes of rebuttal time, began with a response to Starr's discussion of a rational-basis test. She ticked off the kinds of restrictions on abortions that, she argued, such a standard would tolerate and summed up, "That is why this Court must go back to the hallmark of *Roe*. That is, again reaffirm that the right to choose abortion is fundamental. And only when the government can show a compelling purpose—as recognized in *Roe,* that is, a compelling purpose after the point of viability—should it be able to sustain a statute."

The Court deliberated the Pennsylvania law for nearly ten weeks (Savage 1992; Biskupic 2005; Greenhouse 2005). In the process, Justices Kennedy, O'Connor, and Souter coalesced to fashion a compromise ruling. Their joint opinion, from which each of them recited when the decision was announced on June 29, began, "Liberty finds no refuge in a jurisprudence of doubt. Yet 19 years after our holding that the Constitution protects a woman's right to terminate her pregnancy in its early stages, *Roe v. Wade,* 410 U.S. 113 (1973), that definition of liberty is still questioned. . . . After considering the fundamental constitutional questions resolved by *Roe,* principles of institutional integrity, and the rule of *stare decisis,* we are led to conclude this: the essential holding of *Roe v. Wade* should be retained and once again reaffirmed."[9] That result split the Court 5-4.

There was a numerical majority to strike down only the spousal-notice provision of the Pennsylvania law. Like the circuit court, the Supreme Court upheld the remainder of the statute. It had not accepted Kolbert's invitation to reaffirm the principle that abortion rights were "fundamental" and thus that restrictions would have to pass "strict scrutiny"—the strictest constitutional test. The Court substituted the "undue-burden" standard that O'Connor had been promoting from within.

For Kolbert's immediate clients, five clinics and a Pittsburgh doctor, and for the larger abortion rights movement, the judgment on the Pennsylvania law was not what the legal side of the strategy had sought. The State of Pennsylvania had embraced the undue-burden standard, which turned out to be an adequate shield for most of the restrictions it wanted to enforce.

But the case, as Kolbert and her team had imagined it, was really

9. 505 U.S. 844–45.

about *Roe,* even though O'Connor and Kennedy did not think so at oral argument and the Court apparently did not think so when it granted review. Kolbert, unyielding and daring, would not take *Roe* off the table. Her position may well have provoked the Justice Department into rising to the challenge, contributing a legal brief that would be a campaign document used against President George H. W. Bush's bid for reelection.

Not once had Kolbert faltered in her devotion to that strangely worded question, asked publicly the preceding November, "Has the Supreme Court overruled *Roe v. Wade?*"

As she walked out of the courthouse late on the morning of June 29, a half mile away from the hotel ballroom where the strategy had been unveiled, she had her answer: the Court had said no. *Roe*'s "essential holding" remained. Only the justices themselves, especially the trio that controlled the outcome, could say whether Kolbert's argument had set the agenda for the Court's deliberation. A solid, controlled oral argument can do that, even if it is not what the Court expects or wants.

Less than five months later, an abortion rights candidate, Bill Clinton, was elected president. During the campaign, Clinton "was trying to win women's votes by arguing that *Roe v. Wade* hung in the balance" (Biskupic 2005, 266). At least one scholar thought the abortion issue had played a significant role: "Despite the general belief that the presidential election [of 1992] was decided almost exclusively on economic issues, attitudes toward abortion had a significant influence on candidate choice in the overall electorate. . . . [F]ar more 'pro-choice' Republicans than 'pro-life' Democrats defected from their party's presidential candidate" (Abramowitz 1995).

That year, as Kate Michelman had said, it might have been a "winning issue."

Bush v. Gore

Preparing for Oral Combat—the Fight for the Presidency

ARGUED DECEMBER 11, 2000

CHARLES BIERBAUER

Following the U.S. Supreme Court's decision in Bush v. Palm Beach County Canvassing Board (2000)[1] *and concurrent with Democratic presidential candidate Al Gore's contest of the certification of Florida presidential election results, the Florida Supreme Court ordered on December 8, 2000, that the circuit court in Leon County tabulate by hand nine thousand contested ballots from Miami–Dade County. The court also ordered that every county in Florida immediately begin manually recounting all "undervotes" (ballots that did not indicate a vote for president) because there were enough contested ballots to place the outcome of the election in doubt. The Republican presidential candidate, George W. Bush, and his running mate, Richard Cheney, filed a request for review in the U.S. Supreme Court and sought an emergency petition for a stay of the Florida Supreme Court's decision. The U.S. Supreme Court granted review and issued the stay on December 9. It heard oral argument two days later.*

1. 531 U.S. 70.

To listen to passages from oral arguments indicated with , visit www.goodquarrel.com.

FOR ALL THE BALLOTS—CHADS AND DIMPLES, BUTTERFLIES AND absentee, counted or not—the presidential election of 2000 came down to nine votes. The justices of the U.S. Supreme Court did not ultimately vote for Bush or Gore—though partisans may argue that the justices in fact did just that—but rather to decide whether the counting process was faithful to the constitutions of the United States and the State of Florida.

The hastened case, its expedited arguments, and its swift resolution represented the antithesis of the Supreme Court's usual practice, pace, and demeanor. The Court's press corps, much swollen, lined the hallways on the night of December 12, merely thirty-five hours after oral arguments, to receive the Court's sixty-five pages of opinion, concurrence, and dissent. Opinion in hand but without benefit of synopsis, syllabus, or even claim of authorship, we bolted toward our waiting cameras, phones, and computers.

"Page 13," Court public affairs officer Kathy Arberg offered helpfully from her office doorway as we rushed past. Page 13 revealed the clues "reverse and remand," though not the ultimate consequences that would bring the five weeks of postelection suspense to an end.

Going into the December 11 oral arguments, there was no doubt that sentiment at the Supreme Court ran against the Florida Supreme Court's willingness to continue recounting ballots and against Gore's chances of uncovering enough uncounted or miscounted votes to capture Florida's Electoral College votes, which would swing the election to either Bush or Gore.

On the preceding Saturday, the Court had issued a stay of the Florida recounts and granted certiorari for Monday's arguments. *Certiorari* is a Latin word meaning "to be informed of, or to be made certain in regard to." Here it meant that the Supreme Court had agreed to hear an appeal of a decision by a lower court (the Florida Supreme Court).

Gore's attorney, David Boies, believes that his opponent, Ted Olson, "had an easier argument in the sense that he had five judges that had decided his way on Saturday." Olson, looking back, does not disagree. "We thought because of the stay and because of the standards under which a stay can be granted, there were five justices at least who felt there was significant merit to our petition," Olson said in an interview for this book.[2]

Indeed, Justice Antonin G. Scalia signaled what would prove the outcome by writing an unusual concurrence to the Saturday grant of a stay: "The issuance of a stay suggests that a majority of the Court, while not deciding the issues presented, believe that the petitioner [Bush] has a substantial probability of success." And, as Scalia noted, it is unusual for the justices to issue opinions when they are simply deciding whether to uphold a stay.[3]

Yet Court veterans know not to count on presumptions or presume directions. "I didn't assume we had won the game on that," Olson said. "An argument is a little like jujitsu. It's not with your opponent but with the questioner. When you discern a justice interested in a particular area, you respond to their questions."

The arguments in *Bush v. Gore* (2000)[4] took such a turn. To reach federal court jurisdiction, Bush's attorneys had primarily argued against the Florida Supreme Court's permissive counting ruling on grounds that the court had violated the Article II, Section 1 provision of the U.S. Constitution that defers to state legislatures. With regard to presidential elections, Article II states, "Each State shall appoint, in such Manner as the Legislature thereof may direct, a Number of Electors."

In arguments, Justice Anthony M. Kennedy was most troubled by the complexity and potential consequences of the Article II issue arising from the Florida court ruling. "It seems to me a holding which has grave implications for our republican theory of government," Kennedy told Olson. Returning to the point later, Kennedy added, "Because it indicates how unmoored, untethered the legislature is from the constitution of its own state, and it makes every state law issue a federal ques-

2. All quotations from David Boies and Ted Olson are taken from phone interviews conducted by the author for this chapter. The Boies interview took place on August 24, 2006, while the Olson interview was conducted on September 18, 2006.

3. 531 U.S. 1046 (2000).

4. 531 U.S. 98.

tion." He was not unsympathetic to Bush's case, offering what was for Kennedy—and ultimately a majority of the Court—the more palatable argument that Florida's range of ballot types and counting procedures failed to treat all voters equally. As Justice Kennedy also pointed out to Mr. Olson:

JUSTICE KENNEDY: Oh and I thought your point was that the process is being conducted in violation of the Equal Protection Clause, and it is standardless.

MR. OLSON: And the Due Process Clause. And we know is now the new system that was set forth and articulated last."

"You'll recall what happens is that Olson argues entirely the Article II argument," Boies reflects. "There's no mention of equal protection. Kennedy asks, 'What's your federal question?' [Olson] says Article II. He doesn't even mention equal protection." Olson differs to the degree that he says that equal protection "wasn't a fallback" argument: "I felt it was both. It was treating voters in different districts differently. But it was also changing rules after the election."

And what does the justices' line of questioning do for Boies's argument when his turn comes? "Warning bells went off when it was clear Kennedy was trying to push Olson off Article II and onto equal protection. I know I have to do two things. I have to nail down the Article II point, so as not to lose any other justices. Then I have to address the equal protection point." Before Boies could do so, Kennedy dragged him right back to the jurisdictional question dividing the intent of the Florida legislature to qualify its electors by a fixed date from the direction of the Florida Supreme Court to continue recounts, perhaps beyond that so-called safe harbor date.

MR. BOIES: Thank you, Mr. Chief Justice, may it please the Court. Let me begin by addressing what happened in the Beckstrom case that Mr. Klock refers to.

JUSTICE KENNEDY: Could we begin with jurisdiction, first?

MR. BOIES: Yes.

JUSTICE KENNEDY: The Supreme Court of Florida said that it took—that it was cognizant and the legislature was cognizant of 3 U.S.C. Section 5. And for convenience sake, let's call that new law. That's not exactly the—When the Supreme Court used that word, I assume it used it in a legal sense. *Cognizance* means "to take jurisdiction of, to take authoritative notice." Why doesn't that constitute an acceptance by the Supreme Court of the proposition that 3 U.S.C. Section 5 must be interpreted in this case?

MR. BOIES: I think, Your Honor—and obviously this Court and the Florida Supreme Court is the best interpreter of that opinion—but I think a reasonable interpretation of that opinion is to say that what the Florida Supreme Court meant by *cognizant* is that it was taking into account the desire to get the election over in time so that everyone would have the advantage of the safe harbor. I think that goes throughout the opinion.

JUSTICE KENNEDY: Well, the language used in 3 U.S.C. Section 5 is garden-variety language so far as the courts are concerned. We can determine whether or not there is a new law or an old law. That's completely susceptible of judicial interpretation, is it not?

MR. BOIES: Yes, I think it is, Your Honor.

JUSTICE KENNEDY: All right. And it seems to me that if the Florida court and presumably the Florida legislature have acted with reference to 3 U.S.C. Section 5, that it presents now a federal question for us to determine whether or not there is or is not a new law by reason of the various Florida supreme—two Florida Supreme Court decisions.

MR. BOIES: Except, Your Honor, what the Florida Supreme Court did, I think, in its opinion is to say that in terms of looking at how to remedy the situation, it needed to be cognizant of the fact that there was this federal deadline out there that was going to affect Florida's electors if that deadline was not met.

JUSTICE KENNEDY: Well, of course the deadline is meaningless if there's a new law involved. That's part of the equation, too.

"Kennedy and O'Connor continued to ask me questions about Article II. I had to remain on that," Boies recalled, recognizing that there are nine ringmasters at the Supreme Court and that the lawyer at the lectern does not choreograph the performance.

MR. BOIES: I think at that point then you can conclude that what it has done is it has changed the law, but I think the standard is the standard this Court has generally applied in giving deference to state supreme court decisions.

JUSTICE O'CONNOR: But is it in light of Article II? I'm not so sure. I mean, I would have thought that that bears on the standard, frankly, when it contemplates that it is plenary power in the legislature. Does that not mean that a court has to, in interpreting a legislative act, give special deference to the legislature's choices insofar as a presidential election is concerned? I would think that is a tenable view anyway, and especially in light also of the concerns about Section 5.

MR. BOIES: I think, Your Honor, that if the Florida Supreme Court, in interpreting the Florida law, I think the Court needs to take into account the fact that the legislature does have this plenary power. I think when the Florida Supreme Court does that, if it does so within the normal ambit of judicial interpretation, that is a subject for Florida's Supreme Court to take.

JUSTICE O'CONNOR: You are responding as though there were no special burden to show some deference to legislative choices. In this one context—not when courts review laws generally for general elections, but in the context of selection of presidential electors—isn't there a big red flag up there: "Watch out"?

MR. BOIES: I think there is, a sense, Your Honor, and I think the Florida Supreme Court was grappling with that.

JUSTICE O'CONNOR: And you think it did it properly?

MR. BOIES: I think it did do it properly.

"You always would be interested in Kennedy and O'Connor," Olson agreed, as much for their approach to a case as for their judicial philosophy. He separated the Kennedy/O'Connor approach from that of Chief Justice William H. Rehnquist and Justices Scalia and Clarence Thomas. "My guess, and I do not know—underscore that—is that

[Rehnquist, Scalia, and Thomas] thought the structural argument [Article II] was the cleanest, would be less a slippery slope. And they firmly believed that was the sound way to decide the case," Olson said. "But O'Connor and Kennedy tend to multifactored tests and subjective standards."

That's how it came out. Kennedy authored an unsigned per curiam opinion for the Court that reflected his and O'Connor's comfort finding a breach of equal protection in Florida's approach to recounting the votes. Rehnquist, Scalia, and Thomas, perhaps less comfortably, signed on to the Kennedy-authored opinion to reach five votes but added a concurrence that said they would have been more satisfied concluding that Florida's Supreme Court had overstepped its jurisdiction in violation of Article II.

For the record, the vote was 5-4 in favor of the petitioners, Bush and Cheney. Two of the dissenters, Justices David H. Souter and Stephen G. Breyer, were also troubled by the lack of standards in the Florida procedures. "Seven Justices of the Court agree that there are constitutional problems with the recount ordered by the Florida Supreme Court that demand a remedy," the Court opinion said, somewhat deceptively.[5] But Souter and Breyer filed dissents suggesting a remedy other than halting the counting. They would have allowed Florida one more run at a recount, perhaps even beyond the December 12 "safe harbor" date.

The Court's opinion cautions against venturing onto the uncertain seas beyond the calendar's seeming constraint. "It is obvious that the recount cannot be conducted in compliance with the requirements of equal protection and due process without substantial additional work," the per curiam opinion states.[6] Just as Souter had questioned timetable arguments in Court, he contends in his dissent that "the sanction for failing to satisfy the conditions [of a December 12 deadline] is simply loss of what has been called its 'safe harbor.'"[7] Justice Breyer similarly dissents from the insistence on closing the safe harbor gates. He sees lit-

5. 531 U.S. 111 (2000).

6. 531 U.S. 110 (2000).

7. 531 U.S. 130 (2000).

tle risk in venturing into uncharted waters. "By halting the manual recount, and thus ensuring that the uncounted legal votes will not be counted under any standard, this Court crafts a remedy out of proportion to the asserted harm," Justice Breyer states. "And that remedy harms the very fairness interests the Court is attempting to protect."[8]

Olson, of course, had argued that the Florida Supreme Court could not elasticize the timetable.

MR. OLSON: And we submit that [the Florida court] incorrectly interpreted and construed federal law in doing that because what they have inevitably done is provide a process whereby it is virtually impossible, if not completely impossible—and I think it is completely impossible—to have these issues resolved and the controversies resolved in time for that federal statutory deadline. Furthermore, it is quite clear, we submit, that the process has changed.

JUSTICE SOUTER: Well, if your concern was with impossibility, why didn't you let the process run instead of asking for a stay?

MR. OLSON: Well, because we said—

JUSTICE SOUTER: We'd find out.

If Olson had trouble with the timetable, Boies had difficulty with the multiplicity of standards, so varying that the word *standard* seemed oxymoronic.

Summing up "what's bothering Justice Kennedy, Justice Breyer, me, and others," Souter sought to separate the subjective intent of the voter from the observable result and still found problems.

JUSTICE SOUTER: All we have are certain physical characteristics. Those physical characteristics, we are told, are being treated differently from county to county. In that case, where there is no subjective counterindication, isn't it a denial of equal protection to allow that variation?

MR. BOIES: I don't think, I don't think so.

8. 531 U.S. 147 (2000).

Boies's next statement exposed the vagaries of the Florida system, which really did not include clear, uniform objective standards for counting questionable ballots.

MR. BOIES: Maybe if you had specific objective criteria in one county that says we're going to count indented ballots and another county that said we're only going to count the ballot if it is punched through—if you knew you had those two objective standards and they were different, then you might have an equal protection problem.

JUSTICE SOUTER: All right, we're going to assume that we do have that. . . . I think at this stage that there may be such variation, and I think we would have a responsibility to tell the Florida courts what to do about it. On that assumption, what would you tell them to do about it?

MR. BOIES: Well, I think that's a very hard question.

JUSTICE SCALIA: You would tell them to count every vote. We're telling them to count every vote.

MR. BOIES: I would tell them to count every vote.

But of course, the Court was about to tell Boies, Gore, and the Florida Supreme Court that they had no standard, no mechanism, and no time to count every vote.

Every justice would likely assert that the Court acts only in respect to the law. "Don't think of us like those politicians across the street" in Congress, Justice Thomas told a group of high school students on the morning after the Court's decision (ABC News 2000). Still, the atmospherics, anomalies, and politics associated with *Bush v. Gore* were evident in and out of the courtroom. They cannot be ignored here. This was no ordinary case.

Because of the urgency of resolving the presidential election, the issues were expedited to the Supreme Court not once but twice. Like *Bush v. Palm Beach County* ten days earlier, *Bush v. Gore* was argued out of the Court's normal cycle. Each side was permitted forty-five minutes to argue its case rather than the thirty minutes usually allotted.

Chief Justice Rehnquist granted Boies two additional minutes to respond to a question asked as his time ran out. Olson shared ten minutes of his time with Florida attorney Joseph Klock, representing Florida secretary of state Katherine Harris.

The Gore team changed lawyers for the second set of arguments, replacing Harvard law professor Laurence Tribe with Boies, who had been more involved in the cases before the Florida courts. While Tribe had by then argued before the Supreme Court in some thirty cases, Boies had only one prior Supreme Court appearance, *Texaco v. Pennzoil* (1987).[9] Olson, with more than a dozen Supreme Court arguments in his portfolio at that point and more to come as Bush's eventual solicitor general, sees the change of attorneys as a tactical move by the Gore team. "Tribe is, number 1, a professor; an appellate advocate second. His style is professorial," Olson said. "Boies is more of a trial lawyer, effective with the facts, deeply steeped in Florida election law. He was able to make the message that this is about Florida."

The Supreme Court has resisted the notion that cameras have a place in the courtroom. "Over my dead body," Justice Souter has famously repeated whenever asked (Mauro 2006). Souter faced cameras as a justice on the New Hampshire Supreme Court and felt that because of their presence, he pulled his punches during questioning. Chief Justice Rehnquist, also no camera fan, allowed that as long as one justice was opposed, he would not open the shutters. Other justices have worried about television's propensity for chopping complexities into six-second sound bites. Oral arguments are as complex and contextual as can be.

Cameras are not forbidden in federal courts but are treated as a local option. Some years ago, the Supreme Court asked a television network to demonstrate how cameras might be placed discreetly in the courtroom to record proceedings. After the demonstration, the Court thanked the network and never raised the idea again. Correspondents who cover the Supreme Court may bring nothing more than pads and pens to arguments. The quick hands of courtroom artists capture the at-

9. 481 U.S. 1.

mosphere on their sketch pads in the only visual representation permitted.

But for the arguments in both *Palm Beach* and *Bush v. Gore* (and a few cases in the years since), the justices authorized release of the audio that is always recorded, enabling television and radio networks to replay the arguments. Within minutes after Chief Justice Rehnquist declared, "The case is submitted," network audiences could hear his opening words: "We'll hear argument now on number 00-949, *George W. Bush and Richard Cheney v. Albert Gore et al.*" Did the broadcast alter the attorneys' approach?

"In the argument? No, I didn't do anything different," Olson said. "I doubt any advocate would." "When you're in any court, you're just sort of focusing on the judge—justices in this case," said Boies. But looking back, Olson is impressed with the public reaction, immediately and over the years. "People remember vividly listening to the arguments," Olson recalled. "Schoolchildren. Taxi drivers. The uniform reaction I heard was that they were very impressed with the Supreme Court. They didn't realize what we take for granted, that it is a very dynamic, interactive process. And the justices were into it."

Chief Justice Rehnquist, encountering several reporters on the morning after the opinion was issued, allowed that he too was surprised by the level of public interest in listening to the arguments. Boies believes the broadcast added value to the process because it was so widely heard. "From a personal standpoint, I think it was a bad idea for the Court to inject itself into deciding the presidential election," Boies said. "But if the Court is going to do that, it is much better to do it in the open." "The fact it was broadcast may have made the justices a little more polite," Boies ventured, adding, tongue in cheek, "Lawyers are polite in any case."

Klock stumbled when he tried to be too polite by responding to the justices by name. He mistook Justice John Paul Stevens for the late justice William J. Brennan.

JUSTICE STEVENS: What standard would you use in the situation I propose, then?

MR. KLOCK: Well, Justice Brennan, the difficulty is that under—I'm sorry. That's why they tell you not to do that. The standard that is in 166 is in, is dealing with the protest phase, and it was brought about in 1988.

JUSTICE STEVENS: I understand, but my question is if you don't use that standard, what standard would you use for my hypothetical?

MR. KLOCK: The legislature would have to create one, sir. I don't know what standard—

Then he stumbled again.

JUSTICE SOUTER: You are saying that they can't interpret a statute in which there is no explicit definition.

MR. KLOCK: What I'm saying is—

JUSTICE SOUTER: They have to throw their hands up.

MR. KLOCK: No, Justice Breyer. What I'm saying is that—

JUSTICE SOUTER: I'm Justice Souter. You'd better cut that out.

MR. KLOCK: I will now give up. What I'm saying, Sir, is this: that you cannot be in a situation of using the word *interpret* to explain anything that a court does. The word *interpret* cannot carry that much baggage.

Except for the moment of distraction and levity at his expense, Klock focused effectively on the technicalities of the Florida vote-counting process.

Arguing before the U.S. Supreme Court can be daunting and at the same time exhilarating. The courtroom, not terribly large, is typically full for arguments. Apart from those directly involved in the appeal, lawyers observing the case sit in the front, the public in the back, journalists to the side. For *Bush v. Gore,* the Court was crammed with senators from the Judiciary Committee, members of the Gore family, and Washington A-list notables. "The electricity in the Court was so palpable," Olson recalled. "I looked around and said, 'What am I doing here?'" Olson feels that participating in this case was making history, dynamic, and a privilege: "I tell lawyers arguing their first case [before the Supreme Court], 'Turn around and look out there. Where would you rather be? If you conclude that's where you want to be, take a deep breath and enjoy it.'"

Those other lawyers likely will not know for months whether they've succeeded or failed. Only rarely does an attorney find out the next day, as Olson did, that he had persuaded five of the justices to agree with him that the Florida recount should be halted. The rest is political history.

Glickman v. Wileman Brothers and Elliott Inc.

How Oral Arguments Led to a Lawsuit

ARGUED DECEMBER 2, 1996

TONY MAURO

In 1937, Congress passed the Agricultural Marketing Agreement Act (AMAA) to promote fair pricing and uniform marketing conditions in the agriculture business. Exempted from antitrust laws, the AMAA mandated uniform prices, product standards, and other conditions, all of which had to be approved by at least two-thirds of the affected producers and implemented by producer committees appointed by the secretary of agriculture. The AMAA's administrative expenses were to be covered by assessments imposed on activities such as product advertising and promotion. After suffering adverse rulings at the administrative, district, and circuit court levels, a group of California fruit growers, handlers, and processors appealed their constitutional challenge of the AMAA to the Supreme Court.

To listen to passages from oral arguments indicated with 🔊, visit www.goodquarrel.com.

IT IS RARE FOR A SUPREME COURT ORAL ARGUMENT TO BE SO BAD that it provokes a lawsuit. Perhaps the only time it has happened was in an important First Amendment case argued on December 2, 1996.

The case was *Glickman v. Wileman Brothers and Elliott, Inc.* (1997),[1] an appeal in a case originally brought by California fruit growers who challenged a government checkoff program that forced them to pay for advertising they did not like. It was a raucous argument, in which Thomas Campagne, the longtime lawyer for the growers, virtually abandoned his First Amendment claim and became so impassioned about the relative merits of different fruit varieties that he speculated aloud that Justice Antonin G. Scalia was not buying green plums because "you don't want to give your wife diarrhea." Humor usually falls flat at Supreme Court arguments; bathroom humor, even flatter.

Even before the Court handed Campagne a 5-4 defeat, one of the fruit growers was so angry that he sued Campagne for legal malpractice, fraud, and an entirely novel tort: failure to refer the case to a Supreme Court specialist.

The lawsuit ultimately settled without a trial, but the fact that it was filed at all secured Campagne a prominent place in the pantheon of spectacularly unsuccessful Supreme Court advocates. In a broader context, it was also a milestone in the dramatic fin de siècle growth in the dominance of specialists in Supreme Court advocacy.

Campagne served as exhibit A for the proposition that bad things can happen when a local lawyer refuses to give up a case and bring in a specialist as it makes its way to the nation's highest court. That is not to say that specialists always do better. But especially in a case like *Glickman*, where the underlying facts of the dispute faded in importance next to the constitutional issue that the Court wanted to decide, the specialist might have fared better—at least one vote better, which is all Campagne needed to win 5-4 instead of losing 5-4.

There is no doubt that Campagne knew the facts of the case underlying *Glickman v. Wileman Brothers and Elliott*. Since 1983, Campagne, a generalist with a small law firm, had been fighting various marketing

1. 521 U.S. 457.

orders on behalf of a range of agricultural producers. In 1988, he was hired by a contentious group of California fruit growers who objected to a New Deal–era federal law aimed at promoting and stabilizing their industry. Under the law they, like producers of many other crops, were assessed a fee—a checkoff—on the fruit they produced. The money went toward research and marketing projects, including generic advertising that promoted the virtues of their fruit—"Got Milk?" and "Beef: It's What's for Dinner," except for peaches, nectarines, and plums.

The protesting producers objected to paying for ads that promoted varieties they did not grow as well as for more general ads whose tone or message they did not like. One ad of which they disapproved seemed to connect eating peaches with sexual pleasure.

And the fees they were assessed were considerable. One grower involved in the suit said that he paid six hundred thousand dollars per year in fees under the marketing program. Also tangled up in the dispute were rivalries between producers, with some claiming that the advertising favored varieties grown by the farmers who happened to serve on the government board that approved the messages.

After withholding their fees and challenging the program within the agriculture department starting in 1988, the growers took their case to federal court in California. A district court judge dismissed the growers' First Amendment claim in 1993, finding that the mandatory funding of the advertising served a "compelling" government interest. On appeal, however, the U.S. Court of Appeals for the Ninth Circuit reversed and ruled in favor of the objecting producers. The mandatory advertising program violated the First Amendment, the court said, because the government had not proven that its program was better than the alternative—that is, individual advertising produced and paid for directly by the growers themselves.

The government, in the name of agriculture secretary Dan Glickman, appealed to the Supreme Court. The Ninth Circuit ruling, after all, had declared unconstitutional a key component of the government's agricultural policies that dated back to the New Deal, an action that "threatens to have a major impact on the nation's farm economy," according to the petition filed in January 1996 by solicitor general Drew

Days III. The outcome could alter or end more than one hundred federal and state programs that used more than one billion dollars annually in fees for marketing programs.

The appeal also arrived at the Supreme Court at a time when the justices were actively developing their jurisprudence on just how much First Amendment protection is warranted for "commercial speech" or advertising. Another factor in the equation was the Clinton administration's plan to require tobacco companies to pay for advertising against teen smoking. A decision in favor of the fruit growers could affect that campaign. So when the Court granted review (certiorari) in June 1996, the case attracted wide attention.

Cracks soon appeared in the united front of lawyers representing the fruit growers. Until the Supreme Court agreed to hear the case, Campagne had accepted advice from others, and he participated in moot court rehearsals in advance of his Ninth Circuit argument. But when the case reached the Supreme Court, Campagne appeared to hunker down and refuse the assistance of others. Dan Gerawan of Gerawan Farming, one of the main objectors to the program, along with twelve of the sixteen growers involved in the suit, hired a veteran Supreme Court advocate, Michael McConnell, to assist Campagne. McConnell, who has since become a federal appeals court judge, was a renowned expert on First Amendment issues, a professor at the University of Chicago Law School, and a special counsel with Mayer, Brown, and Platt, one of the first law firms to specialize in Supreme Court litigation.

Campagne apparently took offense at McConnell's hiring and, beginning in August 1996, operated on the assumption that Gerawan had fired Campagne, though he continued to represent other growers involved in the case. Gerawan said he did not fire Campagne at all. As the summer wore on, both Campagne and McConnell wrote briefs in the case, and both briefs were filed.

The dispute came to a head in November, when some of Campagne's clients sent him notes requesting that he remain the lead attorney but yield to McConnell for oral argument. On November 11, Campagne responded by in effect firing those clients: "Once you chose Mr. McConnell as your attorney, I could no longer represent you," Campagne told the dissident clients. "In other words, I must inform you that 'you can't have your cake and eat it too.' It's either McConnell or me: not McConnell now and me later." Noting that he had won the case in several lower courts, Campagne said that the clients were making a mistake by choosing McConnell as their advocate.[2]

The two factions' failure to communicate eventually led to an embarrassing impasse. Both McConnell and Campagne filed the routine paperwork with the Supreme Court indicating that they would argue for the respondents in the case, but with only thirty minutes allotted for each side, the high court never allows two lawyers to argue for the same party. Someone had to intervene.

Supreme Court clerk William Suter, whose job includes ensuring that cases are in proper form for consideration by the Court, got the two lawyers on the phone in mid-November to see how the increasingly angry dispute could be resolved. The argument apparently broke out all over again during the phone conversation, and Suter laid down the law. If the two could not agree on who would argue, he would flip a coin. No agreement ensued, so Suter dug a quarter out of his pocket. Campagne picked heads, and McConnell got tails. Suter flipped the coin, and it came up heads. Campagne would argue.

The Gerawan faction kept trying to convince Campagne to step aside or at least accept help from McConnell and other lawyers steeped in the First Amendment doctrine at issue in the case. McConnell forwarded seventeen questions he thought the justices might ask. Seattle lawyer P. Cameron DeVore, probably the leading expert on commercial speech, sent Campagne fifty possible questions. But Campagne apparently completed his preparations without doing any practice arguments.

As the arguments approached, the briefing presented the case as a fairly straightforward test of two main strands of First Amendment law. The first was the so-called *Central Hudson* test for evaluating when regulation of commercial speech is permissible. Based on a 1980 decision, *Central Hudson Gas and Electric Corp. v. Public Service Com-*

2. Letter from Thomas Campagne, dated Nov. 11, 1996. On file with author.

mission,[3] the test said that such restrictions are constitutional if they directly advance a substantial government interest and are not more extensive than necessary. The Ninth Circuit had used this standard to strike down the mandatory advertising fee, finding that the government interest was substantial but that the government had not proven that the program advanced the interest more effectively than the growers could on their own.

The second line of cases had to do with other kinds of compulsory membership. The Court had already resolved disputes in which individual teachers objected to the use of union dues they were required to pay and lawyers objected to the way in which mandatory bar dues were spent. In those cases, the Court said that with limitations, mandatory dues were permissible to advance an important common objective. If that same rule applied to the fruit-marketing program, the law could be rescued.

At ten o'clock on the morning of December 2, Alan Jenkins, an assistant to the solicitor general, rose to defend the fruit-marketing program. "The marketing order provisions at issue here do not ban, suppress, or restrict respondents' speech in any way," Jenkins told the Court. He also said that the program could be upheld under either line of cases but that the bar and union fee cases were "the most analogous" to the case before the Court.

Jenkins deftly handled questions from several justices. Sandra Day O'Connor asked why the government had not pressed the bar and union analogy in lower courts.

JUSTICE O'CONNOR: May I ask a question at an early stage, Mister Jenkins? I think you take the position here that you didn't—that the government didn't argue that the *Abood*[4] line or the union line cases wasn't argued in the Ninth Circuit because of the *Cal-Almond*[5] de-

3. 447 U.S. 557.

4. *Abood v. Detroit Board of Education* (1977).

5. *Cal-Almond, Inc. v. U.S. Department of Agriculture,* 14 F.3d 429.

cision in that court, but the administrative law judge suggests that the government at least in that forum said that the *Abood* line didn't apply, and I'm just wondering if the government has waived that, if we can't just assume that the *Central Hudson* test applies.

MR. JENKINS: Well, I don't—

JUSTICE O'CONNOR: In light of the posture taken below.

MR. JENKINS: I don't think so, Justice O'Connor. In fact, the government has argued throughout this litigation that these programs satisfy both *Central Hudson* and the *Abood* line of cases. We—pardon me.

JUSTICE O'CONNOR: But it does appear that the government below chose not to urge the *Abood* line, took that tactic, and I don't know why we should address that here.

MR. JENKINS: Well, Your Honor, I disagree with that characterization of our position below. I believe that in our briefs in the district court in particular we argued expressly that the *Abood* standard was satisfied and that the *Central Hudson* test was satisfied. It is true that we did not argue in the district court or in the court of appeals that that was the only appropriate test, but I do think that we've argued consistently that both tests are satisfied. In the court of appeals, as you've said, it's true that we were laboring under the adverse precedent in *Cal-Almond,* where the *Central Hudson* test was applied, but we did refer to the *Frame*[6] case from the Third Circuit, which did rely in part on *Abood,* so I think that argument is preserved.

Justice Ruth Bader Ginsburg (and Justice Souter) pressed Jenkins on the mandatory fee line of cases, under which the government must have an important interest that the fee program serves.

JUSTICE GINSBURG: Mister Jenkins, before you do that may I ask you, I think a question that is of a similar basic kind? You latch onto the *Abood* and *Keller*[7] cases. What is the government interest here that compares to the labor peace or the regulation of the bar? That's

6. *U.S. v. Frame,* 885 F.2d 1119 (3d Cir. 1989).

7. *Keller v. State Bar of California* 496 U.S. 1 (1990).

what I don't understand. Why is it so important that we have these orders? What purpose that compares with collective bargaining underlies all of this?

MR. JENKINS: Justice Ginsburg, as I've said, first, the broader interest is in orderly market conditions. I think the legislative history of the Agricultural Marketing Agreement Act, the 1954 legislative history of the adoption of promotional programs, and the record of the formal rule making that gave birth to the advertising provisions of the marketing orders indicate the economic hardship that results and the economic instability in the nation as a whole that results when there's wide fluctuation of market prices, when particularly farmers but other elements of the industry—

JUSTICE GINSBURG: Well, I could understand that if this was across the board, if you said there's this compelling need, and so we do it for all agricultural commodities, but it seems to be rather haphazard.

MR. JENKINS: Well, I think that relates to my answer to Justice Souter's previous question, which is that taking, for example, that one of the proposed disparities is between California-grown peaches and Georgia-grown peaches—and I think it's important to look at the regulatory framework here, which is commodity specific and region specific. Taking peaches as an example: first, California is responsible for the majority of peaches that wind up on people's shelves; but more importantly, between two different regions there are vast disparities in labor costs, in quality.

The length of the season in California is much longer. California-grown peaches have a nationwide market, whereas Georgia-grown peaches are basically locally grown and consumed along the Eastern Seaboard. There are transportation costs that are different. There are investment costs that are different. But I think the particularized nature, commodity-specific nature and region-specific nature of these marketing orders reflects narrow tailoring rather than arbitrariness, but Justice—

JUSTICE SOUTER: How can it be narrow tailoring when the—when in effect the tailoring is done by a nongovernmental entity? I mean, the tailoring to which you are referring, market-specific, region-specific, is simply done by a vote of the people who are growing the peaches.

MR. JENKINS: Well, that's not entirely true, Justice Souter, insofar as the marketing—the Agricultural Marketing Agreement Act treats different commodities in different regions differently, but you're certainly correct that it's the industry in the first instance, a supermajority, two-thirds majority producers, that caused the marketing order to come into being. That's because Congress I think reasonably has determined that people in the industry, operating day to day, are the best measure of need.

Justice Scalia said that similar programs were launched for the same reason for "every industry in the country. It was found not to be true and not to be effective." Jenkins replied that Congress even recently has "reaffirmed the importance of these programs and, in fact, expanded them."

JUSTICE SCALIA: Mr. Jenkins—

MR. JENKINS: Pardon me.

JUSTICE SCALIA: Do we have to believe—this argument sounds like something time-warped out of the 1920s.

JUSTICE SOUTER: The 1930s.

JUSTICE SCALIA: And this is a remnant of the National Industrial Recovery Act, when this kind of an argument was made for every industry in the country, and indeed, they tried to have marketing—the equivalent of marketing orders for every industry in the country. It was found not to be true and not to be effective. Now, do we have to believe it, that somehow it is effective for agricultural marketing orders, but having the government in cooperation with the industry, the corporate state, it is called in Italy, as an efficient mechanism for producing economic prosperity?

MR. JENKINS: I think so, Justice Scalia, for two reasons. First, as we've indicated in our brief at footnote 3, Congress since the court of appeals decision in this case has reaffirmed the importance of these programs and, in fact, expanded them and made significant factual findings regarding their importance, but—pardon me.

JUSTICE SCALIA: Just for agriculture. I mean, Congress hasn't done it for everything else.

MR. JENKINS: Has not done it for every commodity, that's true.

JUSTICE SCALIA: I mean, it seems to express the belief that elsewhere that isn't true.

MR. JENKINS: Well, I don't think so. Again, if I can—

JUSTICE SCALIA: That market disorder is okay; indeed, it's what drives the market.

MR. JENKINS: Well, no, Justice Scalia. I think the determination first is that there may not be significant market disorder and fluctuation in those industries where—private industry where producers have not felt a need to invoke the government's aid, but if I can analogize—

JUSTICE SCALIA: They will invoke the government's aid anywhere. Where have they not felt the need to invoke the government's aid?

MR. JENKINS: Well—

JUSTICE SCALIA: They'll take the government's aid wherever they can get it.

MR. JENKINS: Well, I don't think so. For example, there are a number of commodities for which marketing orders are authorized but where the industry has not chosen to use them, to ask for them. In plums, for example, in 1991, the California—the aspects of the marketing order that relate to plums were terminated because there was an industrywide referendum and plum producers found that it was no longer important. But if I could again analogize to the union context, not every workplace is unionized. It's only where a majority of workers feel that a union will effectuate their interest and therefore Congress's interest in labor peace.

Chief Justice William Rehnquist was also skeptical, suggesting that it would be possible to "organize the market without government advertising."

CHIEF JUSTICE REHNQUIST: Well, isn't it at least, or couldn't Congress find as a fact that in agriculture, at least since after the First World

War, there's always been a problem. If there's a good crop, the prices are low, and if the prices are good, there's virtually no crop. It's a totally different situation from most other kinds of marketed goods.

MR. JENKINS: We think so, Mr. Chief Justice, and I think particularly as to these commodities that is true.

CHIEF JUSTICE REHNQUIST: But that—that could justify the marketing orders, but it certainly doesn't support with any necessity the advertising. You could have marketing orders and try to organize the market without any government advertising.

Again Jenkins pointed to Congress, which has repeatedly determined that generic advertising for agricultural products is beneficial. Jenkins was clearly banking that the Court would defer to a long-standing, well-developed regulatory program enacted by Congress. The fact that some growers disagreed with the content of some of the advertisements did not mean that it violated the First Amendment, Jenkins said; in fact, the First Amendment barely came up in the discussion.

But because several justices seemed skeptical, it appeared possible that if Campagne countered the notion of deferring to Congress with a strong First Amendment argument suggesting that the government was improperly selecting the message of the marketing program, the case was winnable.

But that is not what Campagne did. From the very first, he dwelled on the flaws and disparate treatment of different fruits and different regions under the program. "What is the problem with peaches, plums, and nectarines in California that's any different than the other thirty-two states that grow these commodities?" Campagne asked. Critics later said he should have argued that the fruit industry has no problem that would justify a marketing program under the *Central Hudson* test.

"Disorderly markets are the problem," Scalia replied to Campagne, giving him an opening to reply plainly that there was no proof of disorderly markets. Instead, Campagne launched into a technical discussion of "promulgation records," "Exhibit 297," and "Stipulation 57—I'm sorry, 59," all aimed apparently at showing that the government had not shown that the California fruit market was more disorderly than that of any other region. That irritated Rehnquist, who scolded Campagne, "Just a minute Mr. Campagne. That isn't terribly helpful to simply hold up a brief and say that Stipulation 59—we don't know what—if you want to make a point, make it so we can all understand it." Campagne, barely chastened, said, "Very well, Your Honor," and soon went back to discussing "Exhibit 297."

Now Justice John Paul Stevens was annoyed. "We basically have a constitutional question here, and there are an awful lot of details floating around," he said. "Would it make any difference, as a matter of constitutional law, if Congress had made a finding that this particular market had particular problems that justified this kind of group advertising program? Would you still have the same constitutional argument?" It was a trap, but Campagne did not see it coming. "It would make a huge difference, Your Honor," Campagne said. "They would have an easier time with *Central Hudson.*" That led to the fatal concession. "So you're not saying this sort of program is always unconstitutional?" Stevens asked. "No, Your Honor," said Campagne. "We're not saying that the beef program has to be thrown out, or the milk program." Campagne was clearly seeking to reassure the justices that a victory for him did not mean toppling the full array of government marketing programs. That tactic sometimes helps calm justices who like to move the law along in baby steps, not in sweeping decisions with broad impact.

But in this case, it seemed that by conceding that some marketing programs might be constitutional while others are not, he was giving away his argument. Campagne had turned the case into a quibble over flaws and inequities in one program compared to another rather than one focusing on the basic First Amendment violation committed in all of the programs when the government chooses a message and forces those who disagree with the message to pay for it. As James Moody, one of Gerawan's lawyers, later put it, "There was no doctrinally permissible way to both condemn the tree fruit program while saving other forced speech programs . . . from the constitutional dustbin" (1998, 9).

Several justices immediately pounced on Campagne's concession.

JUSTICE BREYER: We're talking about the First Amendement?

MR. CAMPAGNE: Yes, Your Honor.

JUSTICE BREYER: So what is the First Amendment problem that your client has that wouldn't be shared by anybody who used to fly on the airlines and had to pay money in part for messages that they might have disagreed with that would have been spent by the Air Transport Association required by the Civil Aeronautics Board, or exactly the same thing in the utilities industry, or the trucking industry, or any taxpayer who pays taxes which then is spent by the government on messages they disagree with? In other words, what's the First Amendment interest here that isn't shared in thousands of regulatory situations by millions of members of the public whose money the government often takes to spend, or have other private people spend, on messages that they might not want to pay for?

MR. CAMPAGNE: Your Honor, we would have no objection whatsoever if the secretary of agriculture was taking money out of the General Treasury and—

JUSTICE BREYER: No, no, they didn't—I'm saying the Civil Aeronautics Board, the Interstate Commerce Commission—I mean, I thought the Constitution would permit the public, mistaken or not, to have regulatory systems to regulate every industry, perhaps, if they wanted to, to have a non-free-enterprise system perhaps if they didn't want to. I don't know. I thought those were basically democratic questions. But if we have a system where the industry is regulated, I'm asking what is the First Amendment interest that is different from the same First Amendment interest of every flier, every customer of a trucker, every customer of a utility—I'm just repeating myself, but it seems to me that there are vast numbers of consumers who used to have to spend lots of money they didn't want to spend for messages that regulators would either permit or require.

MR. CAMPAGNE: The First Amendment issue, Your Honor, is two-pronged. First of all, they're forcing us to associate with our competitors, and it's not like the milk board, where milk is white and wet, and so the milk board doesn't have much opportunity to prefer one product over another. When you buy milk, you don't know if it's a Jersey or a Guernsey milk you're drinking, whereas in our commodity, we have over a hundred varieties of plums. My clients happen to grow some green plums. If I tell you today—

JUSTICE SCALIA: Well, then, you would point out, I suppose, that you're not objecting to expenditure of money for advertising or for any other purpose by the government. The United States doesn't contend in this case that these are government expenditures, does it?

MR. CAMPAGNE: No. In their footnote, Your Honor, they admit this is not government speech, although one of their—

JUSTICE SCALIA: So it's not government speech, which would pose a different issue, so we can get rid of a whole lot of those regulatory programs that Justice Breyer was referring to and only limit ourselves to those in which a privately run organization spends money that is assessed against competitors.

JUSTICE BREYER: Namely, all of the programs.

MR. CAMPAGNE: But the point I was trying to make, Your Honor, here we have absolutely no studies whatsoever. When the act was amended in 1965, it was done by one letter, one letter from the secretary to Congress that said, "I would like to implement advertising because—"

JUSTICE STEVENS: It seems to me your argument is they did a lousy job here, but if they'd done a good job, it would be constitutional.

MR. CAMPAGNE: If they could meet the *Central Hudson* test, which was the test they stipulated to before the Ninth Circuit in *Cal-Almond*—

JUSTICE STEVENS: Yes, but we're not bound by that.

JUSTICE BREYER: Why a *Central Hudson* test, where in fact in *Central Hudson* and the other speech cases that seem relevant there was a problem with a person having attributed to him a view that he really didn't hold, and, moreover, an important view, and a political view, and a view of conscience. Is there anything like a political view, a view of conscience, an important, critical view that the public would think that your client held because of these messages?

MR. CAMPAGNE: Yes, Your Honor.

JUSTICE BREYER: What?

MR. CAMPAGNE: Some of our clients testified they don't sponsor lying. They believe—

JUSTICE SCALIA: They don't sponsor what?

MR. CAMPAGNE: Lying. Misleading the public. The generic advertising program is that a California peach is better than a Georgia peach or a South Carolina peach, which together add up to the same amount of volume we have. We say that's not true. There's over a hundred varieties, and if you grow that variety in South Carolina it's going to taste the same as that variety tastes in California. It's a lie. Another one of our clients testified that he really resents the sexual subliminal messages of the advertising board. He happens to be on a hospital board that deals with abuse of children. They—

JUSTICE SOUTER: Is that the picture of this little girl running in a sprinkler eating a nectarine?

MR. CAMPAGNE: And the radio that says so juicy, so sweet, a radio advertisement right afterwards that says eating a peach reminds you of your first kiss in the backseat of your car. He has an ideological problem with that, but more importantly, they're sending a subliminal message that red is better. Now, if I ask each one of you to buy some—

JUSTICE O'CONNOR: Well, there's nothing in words to that effect in the ads, is there?

MR. CAMPAGNE: No, Your Honor. It's the depiction, the subliminal message that red is better, and some of these varieties, not only the Red Jim that you mentioned—

JUSTICE O'CONNOR: Well, would you be here at all if the advertising were in fact generic advertising for California fruit?

MR. CAMPAGNE: Well, first of all they'd have to define to me, Your Honor, in some—

JUSTICE O'CONNOR: Or is there some problem here?

MR. CAMPAGNE: What the problem—that's the point, exactly.

JUSTICE O'CONNOR: Well, what?

MR. CAMPAGNE: I don't know—

JUSTICE O'CONNOR: I'm trying to understand what it is you say causes or results in a First Amendment violation here. It is not clear to me.

Campagne put it as succinctly as he could—one of the few moments when he actually made a First Amendment argument. "They take almost a million dollars a year," said Campagne, "give it to my competitors to advertise fifteen varieties of fruit we don't grow, and force us to associate with our competitors." Justice O'Connor pushed further when she asked, "Don't you represent handlers?" Campagne responded, "I represent handlers/shippers, but there's a big distinction, Your Honor. My handlers are growers who handle their own fruit. The handlers that run the committee are growers who—are handlers who primarily ship fruit grown by other people."

Justice Anthony Kennedy was unimpressed. "Well, of course, you're forced to associate, using your term, by the terms of the marketing order anyway," Kennedy said. "If there were no promotional advertising, you'd be *quote,* "forced to associate," *close quote.* I don't see why the advertising suddenly causes a forced association problem."

Campagne could have replied that by its nature, the forced advertising has First Amendment implications, while other aspects of the association among competitors do not raise First Amendment concerns. Instead, Campagne criticized both Congress and the secretary of agriculture for failing to follow rule-making procedures.

> In 1959, when they promulgated marketing orders for quality control, there was no problem with that. We had no objection to that. But when they moved in 1971 for a legislative amendment and in 1975 and 1976 actually adopted it, with no rule-making record of Congress at all, and then made it discretionary so that annually the secretary of agriculture annually is supposed to be deciding whether to advertise, how much money to advertise, is there a problem in California that's different in other states. He didn't do any of that. Actually, no notice and comment through 1986 harvest, a few months before my trial started.

Once again, O'Connor grew impatient. "I didn't know you were here on some APA claim," she said, referring to the Administrative Procedures Act, which governs executive branch agency procedures. "I thought what we had before us was a First Amendment claim, and I haven't heard a response yet as to what specific problem you have that triggers the First Amendment. Are you relying on the fact that there are assessments made and you have less money to advertise on your own? Is that part of your argument?"

Campagne took another stab, but O'Connor demolished his argument.

MR. CAMPAGNE: That's absolutely what I was trying to express, Your Honor.

JUSTICE O'CONNOR: Well, that's odd, because I thought that there isn't much difference between an assessment or any other fee or tax that government might take, which necessarily, of course, limits your funds for advertising. You have less money.

MR. CAMPAGNE: Yes, but, Your Honor—

JUSTICE O'CONNOR: Do you cite a case from this Court to support you on that?

MR. CAMPAGNE: Yes, *PG & E*, and that is that you're taking our money—

JUSTICE O'CONNOR: *PG & E*—

MR. CAMPAGNE: Yes.

JUSTICE O'CONNOR: Do you have a citation for that?

MR. CAMPAGNE: Yes, Your Honor. *PG & E v. PUC of California*,[8] cited in our merits brief. That's the case, Your Honor, where you struck a rule that required PG & E to promulgate the messages in their own envelopes to others, and the reason this Court struck it is that it stated it would require PG & E to respond when they might not otherwise want to speak, and that's exactly what goes on here. We give almost a million dollars a year, of which 53 percent is devoted to generic collective advertising, to our competitors who grow fruit we don't grow, primarily, and then when we do have a little bit of money left over and try to advertise our own brands, we have to spend a lot of it trying to change the minds of the consumer—

8. 475 U.S. 1 (1986).

JUSTICE O'CONNOR: Do you say that your growers do not—that your clients do not grow peaches or nectarines?

MR. CAMPAGNE: Our clients grow peaches, plums, and nectarines, but there's over one hundred varieties of each peach, plum, and nectarine, unlike beef and unlike milk, where—

For most of the rest of his half hour, Campagne reverted to the argument about which he felt most strongly, even though it had little to do with the First Amendment. In his mind, it appeared, the greatest evil of the forced advertising was that it compelled his clients to pay for ads for varieties they did not grow or like. Not all fruit varieties are alike, so that an ad that features the characteristics of one variety might actually harm the sales of another variety that has different characteristics. "A peach is not a peach," he exclaimed. "A plum is not a plum."

But Stevens saw the flaw in that argument as well. "If this were a homogenous product, you then would not have a problem?" Stevens asked. "That's correct, Your Honor," Campagne said, again acknowledging, in effect, that the fruit marketing program might have been a mismatch for the products it was promoting but was otherwise constitutional.

The argument might as well have ended, but Campagne persisted. His half hour was almost over when he uttered the line that truly made his performance memorable. He had already told the Court that some of his clients grow green plums. But because the forced advertising featured red or purple plums, Campagne seemed to suggest that most people view green plums as unripe. "You ought to buy green plums and give them to your wife," Campagne said, addressing Scalia specifically for some reason, "and you're thinking to yourself right now you don't want to give your wife diarrhea." Amid nervous laughter in the chamber, Scalia sputtered, "Green plums? I would never give my wife a green plum." Unwittingly, Scalia was proving Campagne's point. "I've never even seen a green plum," Scalia said.

Soon, mercifully, Campagne's half hour was up. After a brief rebuttal by Jenkins, the argument was done. But the dispute between the lawyers was far from over. The handlers represented by McConnell were so upset with the argument that on December 4, two days after the argument, McConnell took the unheard-of step of writing a letter to the Court to disavow what Campagne had said (McConnell 1996). The letter, addressed to Suter, told the Court that McConnell's clients "stand by the positions taken in their brief and disavow any concessions made by Mr. Campagne during argument." McConnell added, "To be specific, it is our position that the government does not have authority, under the First Amendment, to decide who will speak for us or what messages will be communicated on our behalf. Contrary to intimations in the argument, our objections are not limited to maladministration of the program; nor do we agree that the program would be constitutional if the advertising were confined to homogeneous products." McConnell asked Suter to circulate the letter to all justices.

"The argument was my worst nightmare," said Dan Gerawan at the time. "I did everything humanly possible to prevent it from happening, but Tom Campagne just refused" (Mauro 1998). McConnell would go no further in criticizing Campagne except to say, "I do not feel as confident going out of the Court that day as I did when I went in" (Mauro 1997). For his part, Campagne portrayed himself as a victim of the sharp elbows of the cliquish Supreme Court bar. "I felt perfectly capable of arguing for 30 minutes on a case that I have lived with for nine years," Campagne said. "There seems to be a club among the Supreme Court advocates, and if you don't give in to the club, they rally together" (Mauro 1997).

The postargument squabble, played out briefly in the press, also did not end the matter. Campagne, anticipating a malpractice suit, beat Gerawan to the punch, suing Gerawan first for breach of contract for failing to pay nearly seventy-five thousand dollars in fees for work on the case. In a letter to the *Fresno Bee,* Campagne said that after he won the coin toss, he "had no option over the matter" and had to argue (Mauro 1997). He also described Gerawan's objections to the oral argument as "an excuse for him not to pay his legal fees." (In his countersuit, Gerawan said that he had paid Campagne more than $1.3 million in legal fees during the prior six years [Mauro 1997].)

Gerawan's lawsuit against Campagne leveled eight charges against him, including malpractice, fraud, breach of contract, and the novel "failure to refer to a specialist." In the complaint, filed in California Superior Court, Gerawan claimed that Campagne "knew, or in the exercise of reasonable care, should have known, that under the circumstances, a reasonably careful and prudent practitioner would have referred [his clients] to counsel with First Amendment expertise and experience in Supreme Court advocacy." The lawsuit raised a number of provocative issues about the importance of oral arguments at the Supreme Court and whether a really bad—or really good—argument can be said to cause the justices to rule one way or the other. Under California law governing negligence suits, Gerawan would have to prove not only that Campagne breached his duty to his clients but that the breach caused the damages—that is, the loss of the case.

In a *Duke Law Journal* article on the malpractice case published while it was pending, managing editor Krista Enns examined the difficult task ahead for Gerawan: "It's a really high hurdle," Enns said in an interview at the time. "You almost have to identify the statement that changed the mind of one of the five justices in the majority."

Enns recounted some of the justices' statements about the importance of oral arguments and the relative merits of arguments made by hometown lawyers as opposed to Supreme Court specialists. Justice Clarence Thomas, for example, has downplayed the importance of oral arguments in making up his mind, while O'Connor has noted more than once that Supreme Court specialists often do no better than generalists do. Rehnquist had cautioned against the use of "hired guns," specialists who may not be as familiar with the record as a lawyer who has been with a case from the start. In a 1972 decision, Rehnquist also wrote for the Court, "We are loathe to attach conclusive weight to the relatively spontaneous responses of counsel to equally spontaneous questioning from the Court during oral argument."[9] At other times, however, Rehnquist has stressed the importance of oral argument at the Supreme Court. "Oral advocacy is probably more important in the

9. *Moose Lodge No. 107 v. Irvis*, 407 U.S. 163, 170 (1972).

Supreme Court of the United States than in most other appellate Courts," Rehnquist said in a 1983 speech. "The opportunity to convince [the justices] of the merits of your position is at its high point" (Rehnquist 1984, 1028).

But how could Gerawan prove conclusively that in this case, Campagne's missteps caused his side to lose? As Enns pointed out, even if Campagne omitted key arguments from his presentation, those arguments were made in the briefs filed by parties and amici curiae (friends of the court) or were aired at earlier stages of the case. Short of subpoenaing the justices and their law clerks, how would Gerawan make his case?

Enns concluded that doing so would be virtually impossible—and possibly undesirable. Having a state court second-guess the validity of a Supreme Court decision might raise federalism issues, she said. And a victory for Gerawan would make general practitioners and hometown lawyers more reluctant than ever to take on Supreme Court cases for fear of being sued for malpractice. "If only a limited pool of attorneys are willing to brief and argue cases before the Court, their services could become too expensive for many litigants, thus restricting access to the Court" (Mauro 1997).

Still, Gerawan tried to make the case. He secured declarations from two key lawyers in support of his causation claim: DeVore, the commercial speech expert, and Moody, one of Gerawan's lawyers, who specialized in challenging agricultural marketing orders (long before Moody made headlines as a lawyer for Monica Lewinsky's erstwhile friend, Linda Tripp). Without hesitation, Moody declared that the 5-4 loss in the Glickman case was "directly and proximately caused" by Campagne's handling of the case, including his refusal to turn over argument duties to McConnell as well as "factual and legal mistakes and concessions" at oral argument. DeVore was more cautious, asserting that the loss was caused "in substantial part by the unresponsive and unsophisticated oral argument made by Mr. Campagne." DeVore noted the oft-repeated maxim among Supreme Court practitioners that "cases in the Court can seldom be won by oral argument but can be lost at oral argument." Campagne's performance, according to DeVore, demonstrates the truth of that maxim.

Were Moody and DeVore correct? Did Campagne lose the case with his subpar argument? It is easy to read the Court's decision in the Glickman case and answer yes. The majority opinion was authored by Stevens, the justice who tried repeatedly to coax Campagne into laying out a clear First Amendment argument against the marketing program. The opinion makes it clear that Campagne's answers never gave Stevens what he wanted to hear. "The legal question that we address is whether being compelled to fund this advertising raises a First Amendment issue for us to resolve, or rather is simply a question of economic policy for Congress and the Executive to resolve," Stevens wrote, adding later, "Respondents' criticisms of generic advertising provide no basis for concluding that factually accurate advertising constitutes an abridgment of anybody's right to speak freely. . . . Although one may indeed question the wisdom of such a program, its debatable features are insufficient to warrant special First Amendment scrutiny."[10] None of the objections Campagne raised to the advertising rose to the level of other cases in which an objector was forced to speak a message that violated his or her political or moral views, Stevens added: "Requiring respondents to pay the assessments cannot be said to engender any crisis of conscience. None of the advertising in this record promotes any particular message other than encouraging consumers to buy California tree fruit."[11]

Campagne's quarrel with the program's treatment of different fruit varieties was also of no consequence to Stevens, who saw it as a "majority rules" kind of program. Stevens wrote, "The mere fact that one or more producers 'do not wish to foster' generic advertising of their product is not a sufficient reason for overriding the judgment of the majority of market participants, bureaucrats, and legislators who have concluded that such programs are beneficial."[12] All of the other justices in the majority—O'Connor, Kennedy, Ginsburg, and Breyer—had also tried in vain to extract a substantial First Amendment argument from Campagne at one point or other in the argument. Could a more per-

---

10. 521. U.S. 457, 468.

11. 521 U.S. 457, 472.

12. 521 U.S. 457, 477.

suasive argument by McConnell have won at least one of them over to the side of the growers? There's no way to say for sure, but it is entirely possible.

Since the *Glickman* ruling, the Court has ruled on several other marketing checkoff cases, ultimately veering away from its reasoning in *Glickman*. Four years later, the Court in *United States v. United Foods, Inc.*[13] struck down a mushroom advertising program on the grounds that it was the main purpose of the government's mushroom regulations, unlike the advertising at issue in *Glickman*, which was but one part of a comprehensive regulatory scheme. That decision gave hope to the opponents of these programs and prompted supporters of the programs to devise new strategies.

So when the Court agreed to consider the beef marketing program in 2005, the government tried out a new argument: instead of viewing it as a case of private speech compelled by the government, it should be analyzed simply as government speech, which the government can control without First Amendment scrutiny. Just as taxpayers cannot object to government messages with which they disagree, the government reasoned, beef producers who pay a fee into a marketing program cannot object to the government-sponsored advertising that results. The Court liked the argument and upheld the program in *Johanns v. Livestock Marketing Association* (2005),[14] essentially removing agricultural marketing programs from the realm of the First Amendment. "The Court's decisions in three mandatory checkoff cases over eight years seem more schizophrenic than schematic," concluded a 2006 article in the *Harvard Journal of Law and Public Policy* (Champoux 2006, 1112).

And what of the malpractice case? A California judge denied Campagne's motions to dismiss the case, finding that at least some of the issues raised by Gerawan should be put before a jury. Perhaps as a result, settlement talks began, and Gerawan reports that the case was settled out of court before trial on terms that cannot be disclosed. Gerawan was pleased with the outcome, though he is still angry about the mar-

13. 533 U.S. 405 (2001).

14. 544 U.S. 550.

keting program, for which he now turns over about one million dollars a year in fees. "Because Campagne was unable or unwilling to coherently present our case, agricultural producers will continue to suffer the burdens of mandatory generic advertising," Gerawan said in early 2007. "I am [still] convinced that had Michael McConnell done the argument, we would have prevailed" (Gerawan, interview by author).

Inside the Court, Suter reportedly has decided that he will never again settle a dispute between lawyers by flipping a coin.

Grutter v. Bollinger

An Argument for the Ages

ARGUED APRIL 1, 2003

GREG STOHR

In 1997, Barbara Grutter, a white resident of Michigan, applied for admission to the University of Michigan Law School. Grutter applied with a 3.8 undergraduate GPA and an LSAT score of 161. She was denied admission. The law school admits that it uses race as a factor in making admissions decisions because it serves a "compelling interest in achieving diversity among its student body." The district court concluded that the law school's stated interest in achieving diversity in the student body was not a compelling one and enjoined the use of race in the admissions process. In reversing, the court of appeals held that Justice Lewis F. Powell Jr.'s opinion in Regents of the University of California v. Bakke (1978)[1] *constituted a binding precedent establishing diversity as a compelling governmental interest sufficient under strict-scrutiny review to justify the use of racial preferences in admissions. The appellate court also rejected the district court's finding that the law school's "critical mass" was the functional equivalent of a quota.*

1. 438 U.S. 265.

To listen to passages from oral arguments indicated with 🔊, visit www.goodquarrel.com.

AMONG THE BEST SUPREME COURT ADVOCATES, A COMMON DEnominator is their intense preparation for argument. Before his appointment as chief justice, John G. Roberts Jr. was one of the best Supreme Court advocates of his generation, in part because of the hundreds of hours he would spend getting ready for his thirty minutes with the justices.

Preparation is the difference between an advocate who can confidently call on an obscure precedent or facts when needed and one who appears to lack command over the subject matter. The prepared lawyer, when confronted with a tough question, has already thought through the logical implications of various responses. Indeed, the best lawyers know most of their answers in advance, having tested them repeatedly before colleagues and at moot courts.

Maureen Mahoney spent months honing her arguments for the University of Michigan in *Grutter v. Bollinger* (2003),[2] a dispute over the constitutionality of race-based university admissions. Retained by the university only after the appeals court arguments, she had to read thousands of pages just to educate herself about the record in the case. She devoted four twelve-hour days to reading the one-hundred-plus amicus curiae (friend of the court) briefs. As is her wont, she created outline after outline, laying out the factual and legal issues, and hundreds of note cards, each with a potential question and her planned answer. She took part in three moot courts.

The university's retention of Mahoney, a partner at Latham and Watkins in Washington, D.C., had been a controversial one in Ann Arbor. Michigan's lead lawyer since the fight began in 1997 had been John Payton of Wilmer, Cutler, and Pickering, also in Washington. Payton was an accomplished black litigator whose specialties included civil rights law. Mahoney was a white Republican with no civil rights background. She did, however, offer significant Supreme Court experience, having served as a law clerk to Justice William H. Rehnquist (before he became chief justice) and later winning ten of the eleven Supreme Court cases she had argued. In an unusual arrangement, Mahoney and Payton

2. 539 U.S. 306.

would share top billing at the high court. Mahoney would represent Michigan Law School in its case, while Payton would defend the university's separate undergraduate admissions program in *Gratz v. Bollinger* (2003),[3] a second argument held immediately afterward.

Together, the cases marked the Court's first look at university affirmative action since its landmark decision in *Regents of the University of California v. Bakke*. Mahoney was asking the justices to declare that campus diversity was a compelling interest that could justify the use of race as a factor in making admissions decisions. She also was arguing that the law school's admissions policy, which considered ethnicity as part of a holistic review of each application, was "narrowly tailored" to meet that goal.

Before Mahoney's turn at bat, however, Kirk Kolbo, a Minneapolis lawyer representing rejected law school applicant Barbara Grutter, was up. Kolbo quickly drew skepticism from Justice Sandra Day O'Connor, who told him that "a university or law school is faced with a serious problem when it's one that gets thousands of applications for just a few slots." Because schools must make choices among those applicants using a variety of factors, she asked, "So how do you single this out, and how are we certain that there's an injury to your client that she wouldn't have experienced for other reasons?" Seconds later, she chided Kolbo for "speaking in absolutes," saying, "And it isn't like that. I think we have given recognition to the use of race in a variety of settings." Kolbo responded simply, "We absolutely agree, Justice O'Connor."

Justice Anthony M. Kennedy followed by pointing to what he called "a broad social and political concern" about an inadequate number of minority lawyers. Kolbo gave no ground, answering that "racial preferences don't address those problems." A few minutes later, Kolbo found himself in deeper trouble when Justices Ruth Bader Ginsburg and John Paul Stevens asked him about a brief, filed by a group of retired military officers, touting the importance of race-based admissions at the nation's service academies. Kolbo responded by taking issue with the premise of

3. 539 U.S. 244.

the question. He noted that the admissions policies at the academies were not part of the official record in the case.

JUSTICE GINSBURG: Mr. Kolbo, may I call your attention in that regard to the brief that was filed on behalf of some retired military officers who said that to have an officer corps that includes minority members in any numbers, there is no way to do it other than to give not an overriding preference but a plus for race. It cannot be done through a percentage plan because of the importance of having people who are highly qualified. What is your answer to the argument made in that brief that there simply is no other way to have armed forces in which minorities will be represented not only largely among the enlisted members but also among the officer cadre?

MR. KOLBO: Justice Ginsburg, I don't believe we have an adequate record in this case from which to conclude that we wouldn't have representation of minorities. The military, in the absence of—

JUSTICE GINSBURG: Suppose that were true. Let's take that as the fact, would you still say nonetheless even if it's true that there will be very few, if any, minority members admitted to the military academies, still you cannot use race?

MR. KOLBO: I believe race could not be used, Your Honor. I think that other solutions could be looked at addressing the problem why there aren't minorities in the military. I note that the United States has not taken a position. We have the brief, as Your Honor has mentioned, from several individuals, [but] the United States has not taken a position in this case, the military academies have not taken a position.

JUSTICE STEVENS: Yes, they have; if the brief is accurate about the regulations, the academies have taken a position.

MR. KOLBO: As I understand it, Justice Stevens, the briefs are filed on the behalf of individuals.

JUSTICE STEVENS: I understand that. But they are quoting material that the academies have distributed which indicate they do give preferences.

MR. KOLBO: Well, Your Honor—

JUSTICE STEVENS: Do you challenge the fact that that is a matter of fact?

MR. KOLBO: We don't challenge what they say, Your Honor. We're just suggesting we don't have a record in this case.

The point was legitimate but trivial, and it angered at least one justice, David H. Souter. "Are you serious that you think there is a serious question about that?" an incredulous Souter asked. "That we cannot take that green brief as a representation of fact." Kolbo extricated himself only with considerable help from Justice Antonin G. Scalia.

MR. KOLBO: I just don't know, Your Honor, what the facts are with respect to the military because this case was—

JUSTICE SCALIA: It depends on what fact you're talking about, doesn't it? You accept the fact that they're giving preferences, but that doesn't convert to the fact that if they didn't give preferences, there is no other way to get an officer corps that includes some minority people. Does the brief say that?

The advocate never did squarely confront the thrust of the retired officers' brief—its argument that racial diversity among the military officer corps was essential for discipline and morale.

Several justices expressed concern that Kolbo's argument might also curb efforts to recruit minority applicants.

JUSTICE KENNEDY: The military brief tells us—the green brief—that there are preparatory schools that the academies have, and 40 percent of the registration in those preparatory schools are racial minorities. And they—suppose the government does this and expends money for the purpose of recruiting and helping racial minorities apply to the academies and succeed there. Is that a proper constitutional purpose?

MR. KOLBO: I see no constitutional objection there, Justice Kennedy. For the reason I think it—it's quite permissible in principle to draw a line between casting a wider net, recruiting, and—and the point of competition where people—where people—where the decision must be made whether people are going to be treated on the basis of the same—

Kolbo tried to draw a line that would distinguish recruitment from selection. The problem for him was that the "point of competition" phrase, which he invoked five times during his twenty-minute argument, had never appeared in his briefs; he was pitching it to the court as a central concept for the first time during argument. And he was less than clear in explaining how that principle might apply to the preparatory schools used by the military academies to help would-be enrollees. He assented when Justice Ginsburg asked whether "you could have minority students only given the benefit of scholarships to go to these preparatory schools." That response forced Scalia again to intervene, asking Kolbo to clarify that he would not allow minority-only preparatory schools.

JUSTICE SCALIA: These preparatory schools—do you concede that they're only for minority students? I'm familiar with those preparatory schools, and they are not.

MR. KOLBO: Certainly not.

JUSTICE SCALIA: The majority of the people that attend them are young men and women who really want to get into the service academies but don't have the grades for it. And the service academy tells them whether they're black, white, or anything else, "Go to these preparatory schools, and you'll have a better chance next time around."

MR. KOLBO: That—

JUSTICE SCALIA: It isn't just for minorities.

MR. KOLBO: They're not, Your Honor. They are open to—accessible to all.

All in all, it was a workman-like performance for Kolbo. He made no major errors, but he stumbled a few times. Most significantly, he missed opportunities to score points with the justices and respond to their concerns. He did little to address O'Connor's worries about his absolutist position or to acknowledge Kennedy's fears about a decline in the number of minority lawyers, much less to make the case that black and Hispanic enrollment at law schools would remain robust. Nor did Kolbo make any real attempt to rebut the case made by the military officers, leaving unanswered the charge that his position would damage national security.

Mahoney's second opponent, solicitor general Ted Olson, had a tough assignment. Olson had pushed internally for the Bush administration to take a clear stance against racial preferences. President George W. Bush refused to go that far, insisting instead on a messy compromise. The government brief praised diversity without saying whether it rose to the level of a compelling interest. At the same time, the administration argued that race-based admissions were unnecessary because of the existence of race-neutral alternatives.

Normally one of the Court's smoothest and most effective advocates, Olson struggled to frame an intellectually coherent position when faced with questioning from Justices Stevens and Ginsburg. Olson waffled on the subject of the military academies, first pointing to a precedent that suggested a limited judicial role in questioning military policies, then refusing to say whether the academies were violating the Constitution. Later, he hedged when Kennedy asked whether diversity was a compelling interest, responding, "The only way to answer that, Justice Kennedy, is that the word *diversity* means so many things to so many different people. . . . If it is an end in and of itself, obviously it is constitutionally objectionable."

As Mahoney rose, she had reason for optimism. The almost-certain swing vote, O'Connor, had signaled discomfort with Kolbo's position. At a minimum, O'Connor seemed open to persuasion. Mahoney, however, still had to tangle with less sympathetic justices—Kennedy, Rehnquist, and especially Scalia. Kennedy fired first, questioning Mahoney when she asserted that Olson had acknowledged that diversity could be a compelling interest. The solicitor general, as Mahoney knew, had scrupulously avoided taking a direct position on that legal question. But Mahoney pointed to ambiguous language in Olson's brief, which discussed the "paramount" government goal of ensuring that public universities were open to all races. And she deftly told Kennedy that the Department of Education had encouraged university efforts to achieve diversity for the past twenty-five years. Her implication was so clear she did not have to make it explicit: If the government was not willing to walk away from twenty-five years of support for diversity, the Court also should not do so.

Rehnquist then directed a hypothetical question to his former clerk, asking whether, in the *Bakke* case, the university could have set aside sixteen seats for minorities after first failing to achieve its diversity goal through other means. Mahoney did not hesitate. In both her brief and preparation for argument, she had developed a clear sense of a line that could distinguish legitimate goals from illegal quotas. Rehnquist's case, she said, would be a quota.

CHIEF JUSTICE REHNQUIST: Ms. Mahoney, supposing that after our *Bakke* decision came down, whereas Cal Davis had set aside sixteen seats for disadvantaged minorities, and Cal Davis said, "All right, we're going to try to get those sixteen seats in some way. We're going to try high school graduates, we're going to try socioeconomic," and none of the—none of those methods get the sixteen seats that they want. Can they then go back and say, "We've tried everything; now we're entitled to set aside sixteen seats"?

MS. MAHONEY: I don't think so, Your Honor. I think what the Court's judgment in *Bakke* said and certainly what Justice Powell's opinion said is that it's simply not necessary to do a set-aside because a plan like the Harvard plan, which takes race into account as one factor, can be used as an effective means to—

CHIEF JUSTICE REHNQUIST: But my hypothesis was, they wanted sixteen seats and that plan just won't give it to them.

MS. MAHONEY: Well, if—if the program was designed to have a fixed sixteen seats, no matter what the qualifications of the applicant pool, no matter what the disparities between the minority and majority students would be, then I think it's fair to say that that would be a quota, if that was the nature of the program.

> But here the record indicates that the—the law school's program is nothing of the kind. That what has occurred over the years with this program is that there have been offers that have ranged from 160 to 232 over the course of eight years; there have been enrollments that went from 44 to 73. It has been a very flexible program.

A moment later, Kennedy asked Mahoney whether the Court would have to defer to a federal trial judge's conclusion that Michigan Law School's pursuit of a "critical mass" of minority students was simply a disguised quota. Mahoney used the question as an opportunity to expound on what in her mind would constitute a quota: "What this Court has said that means is a fixed number that is sufficiently rigid that no matter what the qualifications of the applicant pool, the law school is going to adhere to a fixed minimum." She quoted a passage from the district judge's decision that said the law school "wants 10 to 17 percent of each class to consist of African Americans, Native Americans, and Hispanics." "Wants," Mahoney said. "That's an aspiration. . . . He made no findings that there was a fixed minimum."

Scalia returned to the quota question when Mahoney spoke of ensuring "sufficient numbers" of minorities. "When you say sufficient numbers—that suggests to me that there is—there is some minimum," he said. "Now you don't name it, but there has to be some minimum." Mahoney stood firm. "It can be related to numbers without being a quota," she said.

Scalia pressed again a moment later with the feistiest exchange of the session.

JUSTICE SCALIA: Is 2 percent a critical mass, Ms. Mahoney?
MS. MAHONEY: I don't think so, Your Honor.
JUSTICE SCALIA: 4 percent?
MS. MAHONEY: No, Your Honor. What—
JUSTICE SCALIA: You have to pick some number, don't you?
MS. MAHONEY: Well, actually, what the—
JUSTICE SCALIA: 8—is 8 percent?
MS. MAHONEY: Your Honor, the—

JUSTICE SCALIA: Now, does it stop being a quota because it's somewhere between 8 and 12, but it is a quota if it's 10? I don't understand that reasoning. Once you use the term *critical mass,* you're into quotaland.

MS. MAHONEY: Your Honor, what a quota is under this Court's cases is a fixed number. And there is no fixed number here. The testimony was that it depends on the characteristics of the applicant pool.

JUSTICE SCALIA: As long as you say between 8 and 12, you're okay, is that it? If you said 10, it's bad, but between 8 and 12 is okay because it's not a fixed number. Is that what you think the Constitution—

MS. MAHONEY: No, Your Honor. If it were a fixed range that said it will be a minimum of 8 percent, come hell or high water, no matter what the qualifications of these applicants look like, no matter what it is that the majority applicants could contribute to the benefits of diversity, then certainly that would be a quota. But that is not what occurred here. And in fact the testimony was undisputed that this was not intended to be a fixed goal.

O'Connor so far had been silent. Now, halfway through Mahoney's thirty-minute argument, the justice interjected with her first question. Every affirmative action program the Court had previously approved had come with a fixed expiration date, O'Connor said: "There is none in this, is there? How do we deal with that aspect?" Mahoney later told a reporter that the question, though she had prepared for it, was the toughest of the argument. She knew she had no fully satisfactory answer. Speaking in more measured tones than she had with Scalia, Mahoney implicitly accepted O'Connor's premise that affirmative action programs must be temporary in nature. Mahoney said that in the future, minority applicant pools might be strong enough that universities would not need to consider race. She also said that the experience of being a minority someday might not be so significant in American society. "Have we approved any other affirmative action program with such a vague, distant termination date?" O'Connor asked. "Well, in *Bakke* itself," Mahoney said. She told O'Connor that five justices in that case had concluded that an admissions policy used by Harvard University was constitutional.

O'Connor later signaled interest in the practical implications, asking about the experiences in California, where the state's voters had barred race-conscious admissions at public universities. Mahoney, calling on information from outside the record, described a subsequent drop in black admissions at the state's flagship law school at the University of California at Berkeley. O'Connor then asked about other schools in the state, including the University of California at Los Angeles. Mahoney said that UCLA's graduating class that year included five blacks.

Kennedy returned to the quota issue, making clear that he was not satisfied with Mahoney's approach. He said that Mahoney had given an "improper qualification" in her answer to Scalia. "Suppose the pool is large enough so that you can find minorities to fill your 15 percent aspiration. Why isn't that a quota, even if they're qualified?" Mahoney held her ground. "The difference between a quota and a goal is the flexibility," she said.

As the argument wound down, three friendly justices—Stevens, Stephen G. Breyer, and Ginsburg—all lobbed gentler questions at Mahoney. Stevens asked her to respond to the argument that affirmative action programs created racial hostility. Breyer asked for help in describing what types of admissions programs, in addition to quotas, would be "going too far." Ginsburg asked how Michigan Law School's affirmative action policy had affected Barbara Grutter's chances of admission. Mahoney said the program placed a "very small and diffuse burden" on white applicants. She added that evidence in the case indicated that Grutter would not have been granted admission even in the absence of affirmative action. Scalia got in the final word, telling Mahoney as her time expired that "surely it doesn't make any difference whether she is one of very few who have been treated unconstitutionally." It was a fitting conclusion. All told, Scalia's exchanges with Mahoney had occupied a third of her allotted time.

Mahoney clearly had not satisfied Scalia—or Rehnquist or Kennedy, for that matter. But throughout the argument, she had kept her eye on the crucial vote, O'Connor. Mahoney drew an intellectually coherent line separating quotas from other uses of race. She addressed O'Connor's concerns about an ending point for the program, making a plausible if necessarily speculative argument that affirmative action might not be needed in the future. Throughout, Mahoney provided fodder for an opinion from the Court upholding the Michigan Law School policy.

At least some of the justices were impressed. A moment after Mahoney sat down, Ginsburg leaned over to Souter and quietly shared her assessment. "She's very good," Ginsburg said, in words barely picked up by the Court's recording system. "She's fabulous," Souter said.

Mahoney's argument was the capstone of a high-priced effort by the University of Michigan to preserve colleges' ability to consider race in admissions decisions. The university spent millions of dollars at the trial court level alone to develop a record in support of the value of diversity in higher education. At the Supreme Court, the university's legal team recruited dozens of allies to submit supporting briefs, including key filings by military leaders and Fortune 500 companies.

The efforts bore fruit three months after argument when the Court issued a 5-4 decision upholding the Michigan Law School policy. Although the university's victory was tempered by a loss in the companion fight over its undergraduate admissions policy, the law school ruling gave schools something of a road map for fostering racial diversity. O'Connor's majority opinion said that universities could use race as one of many admissions factors as long as schools considered each applicant as an individual and did not automatically award a "diversity bonus" on the basis of race. O'Connor drew heavily from Mahoney's reasoning. "Some attention to numbers, without more, does not transform a flexible admissions system into a rigid quota," O'Connor wrote. She closed by voicing an expectation that race-based admissions would indeed prove to be a temporary phenomenon. "We expect that 25 years from now, the use of racial preferences will no longer be necessary to further the interest approved today."

For the University of Michigan, however, the case was not the last word. In 2006, Jennifer Gratz, who had pressed a companion case against the university's undergraduate admissions policy, helped put an initiative on the Michigan ballot to outlaw racial preferences at public universities as a matter of state law. Voters approved the measure 58 percent to 42 percent.

Chandler v. Miller

Double Indemnity

ARGUED JANUARY 14, 1997

NINA TOTENBERG

Under a Georgia statute, all candidates for elected state office must pass a urinalysis drug test within thirty days prior to qualifying for nomination or election. Walker Chandler, on behalf of several state office nominees from the Libertarian Party, challenged the statute's constitutionality, naming Georgia's governor (Zell D. Miller) and two other regulatory officials as defendants. On appeal from an adverse district court ruling, the Eleventh Circuit affirmed and the Supreme Court granted certiorari.

To listen to passages from oral arguments indicated with 🔊, visit www.goodquarrel.com.

IN THE MORE THAN THREE DECADES THAT I HAVE COVERED THE Supreme Court, I have seen some wonderful and elegant arguments—and some that are truly wretched.

To pick the worst, we have to begin with definitions. A bad argument does not necessarily mean a losing argument. Nor do a person's legal achievements guarantee a good argument. Attorney general Richard Thornburgh made an embarrassingly unprepared argument in a drug testing case, but he won.[1] And Justice Arthur J. Goldberg, after retiring from the Supreme Court, made such a rambling and pompous argument that he actually asked the chief justice to grant him additional time to finish.[2]

Frankly, it is impossible for me to pick the objectively worst argument I have ever heard; every Court regular has a pet favorite. I can only report what, for me, was the most memorably bad argument, and that is likely because the advocates for *both* sides were so ghastly. The case was *Chandler v. Miller* (1997),[3] argued January 14, 1997. It was brought by three Libertarian Party nominees for office in Georgia who challenged the state law requiring candidates for state office to submit themselves to a drug test before the election. They contended that the drug testing requirement was unconstitutional because it subjected them to a search of their bodies without any specific reason to believe there had been wrongdoing. In particular, they claimed that the state statute violated the Fourth Amendment guarantee that individuals be free from unreasonable searches of their persons, homes, and papers. Among the three was the candidate for lieutenant governor, Walker Chandler, who decided to represent himself at the Supreme Court. Now, it wasn't that he or his co-plaintiffs could not afford an attorney. He spurned offers of help from various civil liberties groups and sallied forth on his own, proving at oral argument the old maxim that only a fool has himself for a lawyer.

---

1. *Skinner, Secretary of Transportation et al. v. Railway Labor Executives' Association et al.*, 489 U.S. 602 (1989).

2. *Flood v. Kuhn*, 407 U.S. 258 (1972).

3. 520 U.S. 305.

Thirty seconds into Chandler's argument, the justices began, quite simply, to tear him to shreds. Totally unprepared, Chandler had the aura of a sleepwalker. At his opening, he wasted valuable minutes because he could not answer Justice Sandra Day O'Connor's questions on whether his case was moot. (Justice Anthony M. Kennedy and Chief Justice William H. Rehnquist also entered the discussion of this issue.) Chandler survived that episode thanks only to a rescue operation launched by Justice Antonin G. Scalia.

JUSTICE O'CONNOR: Mister Chandler—

MR. CHANDLER: Yes.

JUSTICE O'CONNOR: You say that the petitioners ran for office in [1994,] and in the petition you brought here, there's no assertion that any of the petitioners plan to run again in the future, is there?

MR. CHANDLER: Not in the—as I recall, not in the actual pleadings in the lower court. However—

JUSTICE O'CONNOR: No. So how would we have jurisdiction?

MR. CHANDLER: Your Honor, I believe this case would not be moot, because it would be capable of repetition and yet evading—

JUSTICE O'CONNOR: Well, how would it be if none of the petitioners plan to run again?

MR. CHANDLER: Your Honor, I plan to run again.

JUSTICE O'CONNOR: But that was not stated.

MR. CHANDLER: That was not stated below. Also, Justice O'Connor, I—my candidacy and the candidacy of all Libertarian Party members is premised on the concepts of limited government and freedom from unconstitutional searches and seizures among all the other liberties reserved to the people by the Founding Fathers, and in that respect I would think that OCGA 21-2-140 is violative of the interests of all candidates, whether or not—

JUSTICE O'CONNOR: Well, that's a merits argument, certainly, but normally we would look to see if there's some situation in a case like this of being capable of repetition and avoiding any review, and normally we would look to see some avowal that yes, indeed, these petitioners or at least one of them intends to run again.

MR. CHANDLER: Yes, I understand that.

JUSTICE KENNEDY: And you didn't seek to bring this on behalf of a class of candidates.

MR. CHANDLER: No, Sir, Your Honor, I did not.

CHIEF JUSTICE REHNQUIST: Mr. Chandler?

MR. CHANDLER: Yes.

CHIEF JUSTICE REHNQUIST: I'm wondering why, if you want to raise this issue, you don't have to refuse to take the drug test rather than go ahead and take it and get on the ballot and then challenge it later.

MR. CHANDLER: Your Honor, we filed this action prior to submitting to the test, prior to qualification by having this little piece of paper that certified us as being drug-free. We were the nominees of our party. We had an obligation to take forward the message of our party, the other messages of our party in the electoral process, so we essentially had no choice but to submit—unwillingly, perhaps, but to submit to this state-ordered search.

JUSTICE SCALIA: When did you file the suit, before the election or after the election?

MR. CHANDLER: Before the election, Your Honor, in May of—

JUSTICE SCALIA: So at that time, there's no doubt that the case was not moot.

MR. CHANDLER: Yes, Your Honor.

JUSTICE SCALIA: At that time it was very much alive.

MR. CHANDLER: Yes, Your Honor.

JUSTICE SCALIA: So the complaint is that you—what, that you didn't amend your complaint in order to assert repetition after the election? Have we ever required that, amending a complaint in a suit that originally was not moot in order to aver that mootness has not occurred?

MR. CHANDLER: I don't know, Justice Scalia.

JUSTICE SCALIA: I don't recall we've ever required that.

Justice Kennedy led off the next line of interrogation, asking whether it would be an unconstitutional search if the state required all of its employees to have a physical exam with the results going only to the patient. Chandler misunderstood the question and said that such a requirement would be unconstitutional because an employee might lose his job as a result.

JUSTICE KENNEDY: Suppose that a state agency said, "In the interests of all of our employees, everyone once a year must take a physical exam. We don't want to know the results. All we want you to do is to say that you've gone to a doctor, any doctor you want, for a physical examination." Is that a search?

MR. CHANDLER: Yes, Your Honor, I would think that would be a search.

JUSTICE KENNEDY: When does a search arise? When you go into the doctor's office?

MR. CHANDLER: I would think so, Your Honor.

JUSTICE KENNEDY: Even though the results are disclosed only to you?

MR. CHANDLER: I would think that it would be a search, because if the result of that search is that you can no longer serve in that agency, then—

"No, no, no," said Kennedy, repeating that the results would be given only to the patient. A befuddled Chandler responded, "With all due respect, that's not before the Court."

Kennedy, now adopting a tone he might use for a five-year-old, explained that "there are a lot of things that are not before the Court that are going to be before the Court based on this opinion, and so we have to write an opinion that covers more than your particular case because we're interested in the general principle." Chandler had difficulty answering.

MR. CHANDLER: Yes, Your Honor. I—

JUSTICE KENNEDY: So I'm asking, why is this a search?

MR. CHANDLER: I would think that it would be a search if, as a result of that search, a person could lose employment.

JUSTICE KENNEDY: That's not my hypothetical. All you have to do is go to the doctor and just certify that you've had a physical exam once a year at a doctor of your choice. The agency says, "We want to do this in the interests of our employees," and that may well—we can play with the hypothetical.

MR. CHANDLER: Yes, Sir.

JUSTICE KENNEDY: The agency pays for it, or whatever. Why is that a search?

Struggling to answer the question, Chandler mangled the name of a key legal precedent on which he was relying and finally conceded that perhaps a mandatory physical exam once a year is not a search.

MR. CHANDLER: I would think it would be a search under the principles of—that were announced in *Schermberger*, which drew a distinction between bodily searches—

JUSTICE KENNEDY: That is to say, *Schmerber*?[4]

MR. CHANDLER: Yes, Sir.

JUSTICE KENNEDY: Well, there the—involuntarily a needle was inserted in the—with the patient by a doctor who was not of his choice at a time that was not of his choice. He had—he was there, on the gurney, in custody. But that's quite different, it seems to me, from just saying, "Go to a doctor once a year."

MR. CHANDLER: It may well be, Your Honor.

At that, Justice Scalia pounced.

JUSTICE SCALIA: It may well be? You think—I assume this physical exam requires a strip, right?

MR. CHANDLER: Yes, Sir.

JUSTICE SCALIA: And you're saying that that's not a search, requiring you to go to somebody else and strip down and have that person examine your body?

MR. CHANDLER: I think it's—

JUSTICE SCALIA: What possibly could be a search if that's not a search?

4. 384 U.S. 757 (1966).

MR. CHANDLER: Yes, Your Honor.

JUSTICE SCALIA: I mean, you might want to argue about whether it's an unreasonable search, but you don't have any doubt it's a search, do you?

MR. CHANDLER: No, Sir, Your Honor.

Justice O'Connor now asked whether Chandler would have any problem if the state required an affidavit from candidates attesting to the fact that they were not now using nor had they ever used drugs. Chandler came up dry.

JUSTICE O'CONNOR: Mr. Chandler, would you have any problem if what the state did instead of requiring a drug test within thirty days of filing your nominating petition is require every candidate for the state office to file an affidavit certifying that the candidate is not now and has not in the past used or ingested illegal narcotic drugs?

MR. CHANDLER: I would object to that, Your Honor, because that would—

JUSTICE O'CONNOR: There's no search.

MR. CHANDLER: There is no search, but I—

JUSTICE O'CONNOR: It certainly wouldn't—you wouldn't be here on the basis that you are here today.

MR. CHANDLER: That would be true.

JUSTICE O'CONNOR: And a state has wide latitude, does it not, to define qualifications for state office?

MR. CHANDLER: Yes, so long as those—so long as they do not violate people's constitutional protections.

JUSTICE O'CONNOR: And what constitutional protection would be violated by requiring such an affidavit, that to be a candidate for state office you certify that you're not a drug abuser?

MR. CHANDLER: Or never have been, in your hypothetical, Your Honor. You asked if I would object, and I would object not on constitutional grounds—

JUSTICE O'CONNOR: I'm asking on what constitutional basis.

MR. CHANDLER: I'm sorry, Your Honor, I fail to know of a constitutional basis that that might fit within that hypothetical.

O'Connor, her foot all but tapping beneath the bench, closed her line of questioning, and Chandler remained at a loss.

JUSTICE O'CONNOR: You just wouldn't like it.

MR. CHANDLER: Yes. I think that it might have some implication for free—free speech implications under the First Amendment, Your Honor, but—

Justice Ruth Bader Ginsburg then moved on to another hypothetical: Would Chandler object to a complete financial disclosure for all candidates? Chandler said he would not and did not. Ginsburg observed that the Fourth Amendment protects private papers as well as persons.

JUSTICE GINSBURG: But the Fourth Amendment does say persons, houses, papers, so why would you say that it's all right to demand papers but not have anything to do with the person?

Chandler did not have an answer that satisfied Ginsburg.

MR. CHANDLER: Because I think there is a strong, compelling privacy interest in the person that goes far beyond the compelling—any compelling interest.

JUSTICE GINSBURG: Where do you get that in the Constitution?

MR. CHANDLER: Justice Ginsburg, I do not know.

JUSTICE KENNEDY: And is the personal interest in not having to strip and have needles inserted, or is it the personal interest in not disclosing the results, because if it's the latter, then your case is perhaps more difficult.

MR. CHANDLER: I think it's the former, your honor. It's the actual giving up of bodily fluids, the insertion of—

JUSTICE KENNEDY [*incredulous*]: So you think most people would think that that's more of an invasion of privacy, just going to the doctor once a year, than having to disclose all of your financial records, all of your holding, all of your poverty or all of your wealth, as the case may be?

Justice Scalia tried to help out Chandler a bit, observing that not every search is unreasonable, but Chandler got tangled up, asserting that even orally disclosing drug use amounted to an illegal search.

JUSTICE SCALIA: Mr. Chandler, every invasion of privacy is not a search, is it? Are you willing to equate every invasion of privacy with a search? I mean, would you consider it a search if, instead of having someone examine you physically to decide whether you have cocaine in your body, you are required to disclose whether you have cocaine in your body? I mean, that may be an invasion of privacy, but is it a search?

MR. CHANDLER: Yes, Sir, I would deem it a search.

That prompted Justice O'Connor to interject, "You just told me it wasn't, so which answer are you giving? You answered to me that 'No, it wouldn't be a Fourth Amendment search, but I'd object,' and now you tell Justice Scalia, 'Yes, it's a search.' Now, which answer do you want to abide by here?" A pathetic Chandler replied, "I'm sorry, Justice O'Connor. I'm not exactly sure of the contradiction that I've voiced here."

Justice David H. Souter now threw a lifeline to Chandler, adopting the soothing tone parents reserve for talking to upset children: "All right, and what is your reason for saying that this particular search is not a reasonable one? What's the nub of your attack on the government's justification?" And here, three-quarters of the way through his time, Chandler finally got to the heart of things. The Court, he noted, had upheld drug tests in cases where there was a demonstrated need—for people handling firearms or running trains, for example—but in this case, he said, "There is no real evidence of a real problem." Georgia's drug testing law, he said, is a "blanket search carried out for symbolic purposes" to show that the state is against drug use.

That answer goosed Chief Justice Rehnquist: "Don't you think there is an argument on behalf of the state that the people have a right to have a lieutenant governor who is free of drug use?" Chandler's first answer was that one of his co-plaintiffs was not running for lieutenant governor but agriculture commissioner. Only after that did he get to what should have been his first and only answer: There never had been any showing of drug use or abuse in high office in Georgia.

Could the situation deteriorate even further? Oh, yes. Could the state disqualify someone from being governor if he or she were found to be using drugs? Chandler said even that would be a problem for him. Justice Kennedy then asked whether it would be all right for a governor to be using illegal drugs. Chandler's answer: it would depend on the frequency and which drugs.

JUSTICE KENNEDY: You'd have no problem with the law saying—that maybe you do, but if a high official—say, the governor—uses drugs, he is immediately disqualified from office—illegal drugs?

MR. CHANDLER: Your Honor, for one thing, that—

JUSTICE KENNEDY: Would you have a problem with that?

MR. CHANDLER: I would even have a problem with that, Your Honor.

JUSTICE KENNEDY: Why?

MR. CHANDLER: For one thing, that presupposes that the person that's in the high office has broken the laws of the State of Georgia. The person could have, for example, been in a jurisdiction or another country where such drug use was not even illegal. Therefore, he would not have broken the laws under the State of Georgia. It is a shifting majority [that] decides what is legal and illegal. We see tobacco, for example, approaching illegality in this country, or portions thereof. That introduces the novel idea that a citizen of a state is subject to the jurisdiction of that state no matter where in the world he or she might go, and that is an element—

JUSTICE KENNEDY: You think drug use is irrelevant to the abilities and the qualifications of a public officeholder?

MR. CHANDLER: Your Honor, I would think that that would be a matter of a question of how long ago was it, the frequency of use—

JUSTICE KENNEDY: Let's just suppose, during his term of office.

MR. CHANDLER: During his term of office, Your Honor, again it might be a question of frequency. It might be a question of which drugs are being talked about. It might be—there might be any number of questions.

Battered and bloody, Chandler reserved the remaining five minutes of his time for rebuttal.

And now it was time for the state's lawyer, assistant attorney general Patricia Guilday, to self-immolate. She knew that mootness was a question about which some justices were concerned because she had the advantage of having heard those questions put to her opponent. Moreover, if the case were moot, the state law would remain intact. But she was just as befuddled about the issue as Chandler was and used up the first precious six minutes of her argument—one-fifth of her time—demonstrating her confusion, admitting at one point that she was not sure how to read the Court's previous decisions in this area.

MS. GUILDAY: We read closely this Court's opinion in *Storer, Norman, Meyer v. Grant,* and the *Democrat Party v. Wisconsin,* all of which were elections cases.[5] There were various factual contexts in those cases, and in many, or in some at least, the facts were similar, where the election was over and there was no statement that the particular candidates intended to run for office in the future. Nonetheless, this Court held that because it was an elections context and the issues were likely to come before the Court again, that—I'm not sure which way to read the Court, either. It was not moot, and so we will hear it, or it is moot, but even though it is moot we are going to consider it because it is an elections context.

Moving on to the merits of the case, Guilday conceded under questioning from Justice O'Connor that there was no record in the state of Georgia of drug use being a problem with officeholders, and when pressed to provide some justifying special need to drug test candidates, Guilday could cite only the fact that elected public officials are trustees of the public and have fiduciary responsibilities.

JUSTICE O'CONNOR: Ms. Guilday, may I ask you whether there is any place in the record in this case where we might find evidence of some

5. 415 U.S. 724 (1974), 502 U.S. 279 (1992), 486 U.S. 414 (1988), and 450 U.S. 107 (1981).

particular or special need in Georgia for a suspicionless general search program for candidates for office in Georgia? Is there any place where, in this record, we might find that, oh, there have been a number of officeholders, state officeholders in Georgia, who have turned out to have drug problems?

MS. GUILDAY: There is no such record evidence in this case, Your Honor.

JUSTICE O'CONNOR: And was any offered by the state and rejected?

MS. GUILDAY: No, Your Honor. The reason there was not—and I'm not sure at what stage you're talking about. At the time the legislature passed this statute—Georgia law has consistently held from the beginning that in Georgia, the statute itself evidences the legislative history. There is no recording of any committee hearings, of any floor debate, anything like that.

JUSTICE O'CONNOR: Is there any indication anywhere in this record that Georgia has a particular problem here with state officeholders being drug abusers?

MS. GUILDAY: No, there is no such evidence, Your Honor, and there is no—to be frank, there is no such problem as we sit here today.

JUSTICE O'CONNOR: Has this Court, in dealing with suspicionless searches, looked to what special needs there might be that would be an indication that a suspicionless—a blanket, suspicionless search would be appropriate? Isn't that what we've looked to? Is there a special need for the government?

MS. GUILDAY: I think the question as to whether there is a special—

JUSTICE O'CONNOR: Have we looked to that, or not? *Von Raab*[6] or other cases on which you rely—has this Court looked at a special need by the government—

MS. GUILDAY: Absolutely.

JUSTICE O'CONNOR: —for a suspicionless search program?

MS. GUILDAY: Absolutely, the Court has looked at special need.

JUSTICE O'CONNOR: Okay. So what is the need Georgia asserts here that is special?

---

6. 489 U.S. 656 (1989).

MS. GUILDAY: The special need that Georgia asserts is that in Georgia the elected officials that are included in this statute are by constitution trustees and servants of the public.

Noting that many states require candidates to make financial disclosures, Justice John Paul Stevens asked whether a candidate's papers could be searched to ensure compliance with those disclosure laws. "No," responded Guilday, "that would not be permissible." Stevens, along with Justice Souter, continued in this line of questioning a short time later.

JUSTICE STEVENS: And your reason for saying, this is different, is that the search is less intrusive?

MS. GUILDAY: Exactly, just as this Court has held in *Skinner, Von Raab,* and *Acton.*[7]

JUSTICE SOUTER: Because it is a body search as opposed to a paper search?

MS. GUILDAY: I don't think the distinction is body versus paper. I think the distinction is what information is disclosed.

Souter pressed the point further with a hypothetical.

JUSTICE SOUTER: Well, what about a case—let's take a building search. I suppose the state has just as much interest in assuring itself that its candidates and its officers are not drug possessors and drug dealers as it has in assuring them that they are at least not current drug users. Would it violate the Fourth Amendment to require a candidate to open his house to a search by some private investigatory agency which would then certify after the search that no drugs were found there? Would that violate the Fourth Amendment?

MS. GUILDAY: I believe it certainly would violate the Fourth Amendment.

JUSTICE SOUTER: And why is opening the house less intrusive than opening the body?

7. 489 U.S. 602 (1989), 489 U.S. 656 (1989), 515 U.S. 646 (1995).

Grasping at straws, Guilday soon reverted to a states' rights argument, citing the Tenth Amendment and asserting that it instructs the Courts to defer to the states on ballot restriction questions as long as these state laws do not invade an individual's fundamental rights. Chief Justice Rehnquist dryly commented, "I wouldn't have thought you could derive all of that from the Tenth Amendment. It doesn't say anything about ballot restrictions that I know." Justice Souter added that he did not understand Guilday's Tenth Amendment argument: "I take it you do not argue that the Tenth Amendment in effect gives the states some kind of right or some—dispensation from the Fourth Amendment, so what is the Tenth Amendment argument?"

Guilday's other major challenge came from Justice Stephen Breyer, who wondered about the effectiveness of a drug test taken anyplace the candidate wishes and anytime he wishes as long as it is within the thirty-day period before the election. Opined Breyer, "You find one day where you go in and you're drug-free. All right, so how's that supposed to prove anything? I mean, I guess the greatest druggie in the world could go in and find a day when he was drug-free [and could pass the test]." Guilday conceded that foiling the test would be easy. So Breyer asked about the state's justification for the statute: "What is the theory behind the statute other than making a political statement?" Guilday's answer was gibberish: "In our case, the primary purpose we would offer this Court for this statute is that the information that a negative drug test gives to the public about the individual candidate is significant." Adding insult to injury, Guilday implied that the Georgia Assembly had passed this law on a whim, with no evidence, no hearings, and no findings of any kind.

Justice Ginsburg observed that since the testing system was not random and could have no reasonable expectation of catching drug users, it was little more than a symbolic statement by the state legislature. In choosing between a political statement and a constitutional provision, the justice asked with a wry smile, "doesn't the Fourth Amendment always win?"

After Guilday had finished her argument, Chandler returned to the lectern for his rebuttal. Perhaps it was watching his opponent get slammed as hard as he had been, or maybe he was just slaphappy, but he seemed to do a little better in his last few minutes by appealing to the judicial sense of humor. When he reiterated that there was no evidence of drug use by Georgia lieutenant governors or agriculture commissioners, Chief Justice Rehnquist asked why the state had to wait for a problem to arise in Georgia. What if there already were a lieutenant governor and an agriculture commissioner on drugs in Alabama? Replied Chandler, "A lot of things happen in Alabama that don't happen in Georgia." Justice Scalia joined in the spirit of the moment, asking whether the state would have to justify drug testing by showing that the commissioner of agriculture did a worse job because of his drug habit. "I mean," Scalia quipped, "It's supposed to be good for poetry." Replied Chandler, "And also your Honor, how could we argue that drug users would be any worse than the General Assembly Georgia has now?"

In the end, both Chandler and Guilday stumbled across the finish line only by virtue of having physically survived the argument. In any intellectual sense, they were both dead meat.

P.S. The Court ruled unanimously in Chandler's favor.

Rapanos v. United States

Wading into the Wetlands

ARGUED FEBRUARY 21, 2006

DAVID G. SAVAGE

John Rapanos sought to fill in three wetland areas on his property to build a shopping center. Rapanos ignored warnings from the Michigan Department of Environmental Quality that the area was protected wetlands under the Clean Water Act (CWA). The CWA allows the government to regulate the discharge of any pollutant (including dirt or sand) into "navigable waters," which the act defines as "the waters of the United States." Under regulations issued by the Army Corps of Engineers, wetlands are covered by the CWA as long as they are adjacent to traditionally navigable waters or tributaries of such waters. After Rapanos also ignored cease-and-desist orders from the U.S. Environmental Protection Agency, the government brought a civil suit against him. Rapanos argued before the district court that the CWA gives the government jurisdiction to regulate only traditionally navigable waters. The district court rejected Rapanos's argument and upheld the corps's regulations including the wetlands as "waters of the United States." The Sixth Circuit Court of Appeals affirmed.

To listen to passages from oral arguments indicated with 🔊, visit www.goodquarrel.com.

"YOU WIN SOME. YOU LOSE SOME," SAID FORMER VICE PRESIDENT Al Gore at the 2004 Democratic National Convention. "Then there's that little-known third category."

Lawyers who practice regularly before the Supreme Court are familiar with that category. They win some and lose some, but in a surprising number of cases, it is not entirely clear who won and who lost. Often, both sides claim victory because, they say, the Court's decision—or the wording of its opinion—gave them what they wanted.

Of course, the lawyers don't decide the cases or determine how they are decided. In the end, the justices—perhaps as few as five of them—decide a case based on their view of the law at issue, not on how the case was presented to them. But the lawyers have a chance to persuade the justices to adopt a particular rule of law. That in turn requires the lawyers to think through and to explain how this rule will work in practice. At their best—and in the closest cases—effective lawyers can tip the balance by reassuring a wavering justice (or several) that there is a right answer to the legal question before them.

Federal Power and Water Rights

The first and oldest question in American constitutional law concerns the reach of the federal government's power. In 1787, the drafters of the Constitution sought to give the newly reformed national government certain but not all powers. Their opponents—the Antifederalists—were not reassured. They feared that the national government would claim ever more power and threaten the liberty of its citizens. The Supreme Court got under way a few years later and has spent much of its time since then trying to answer versions of the same question: What is the limit on federal power?

If there is indeed a limit, John Rapanos certainly thought he and Michigan farm fields lay well beyond it. He owned 230 acres near Midland, about twenty miles from Lake Huron. Several acres were marshy and low-lying. When it rained, water flowed from there to a drainage ditch and then to Hoppler Creek, which in turn flowed into the Kawkawlin River, which emptied into Lake Huron.

In 1988, Rapanos said that he planned to clear the land so it could be developed for a shopping center. He had similar plans for two other nearby parcels of land. However, state and federal regulators warned him that there were wetlands on his land and that he could not proceed without obtaining a permit. The Clean Water Act of 1972 made it illegal to put "any pollutant" into the "waters of the United States" without a permit. The act defined *pollutant* to include not just sewage and toxins but also dredged or fill material such as rock, sand, or dirt. And it defined *waters of the United States* as "navigable waters."

No one would claim that the marshy spots on this farmer's field were "navigable." But water flows downhill, and since the 1970s, the Environmental Protection Agency and the U.S. Army Corps of Engineers has insisted that wetlands were part of the "waters of the United States" because filling (or polluting) them would damage America's lakes and rivers. Since wetlands were a kind of natural sponge, they also helped to control floods and erosion. Despite repeated warnings from the Michigan regulators and the U.S. Environmental Protection Agency, Rapanos hired bulldozers to push sand and gravel into more than fifty-four acres of wetlands on his three parcels of land. So began what became the Supreme Court case of *Rapanos v. United States* (2006).[1]

Along the way, Rapanos and his battle with federal regulators became a cause célèbre for the property rights movement. The Michigan developer was prosecuted on criminal charges and was hit with more than ten million dollars in fines. He lost at every stage in the lower courts. The Sixth Circuit Court of Appeals reasoned that since "a hydrological connection" existed between the wetlands on his property and the Great Lakes, federal regulators had the authority they needed to stop him from filling the marshes. Despite his losses, Rapanos found a well-funded champion in the Pacific Legal Foundation (PLF) in Sacramento, California, which defends property rights. Its lawyers took up his appeal. The group had long complained about overreaching by the

1. 547 U.S. 715.

Army Corps of Engineers, and it won a sympathetic hearing from the Rehnquist Court.

Setting the Stage for Rapanos

After law school at Stanford University, both William H. Rehnquist and Sandra Day O'Connor settled in the Phoenix area, and both came to the Supreme Court with a conservative westerner's skepticism toward federal regulators. They agreed with Justices Antonin G. Scalia, Anthony M. Kennedy, and Clarence Thomas that the Constitution put limits on federal power, and in 2001, Rehnquist spoke for a 5-4 majority in *Solid Waste Agency of Northern Cook County (SWANCC) v. U.S. Army Corps of Engineers*[2] that held that "isolated" ponds and wetlands lay beyond the regulatory authority of the Army Corps of Engineers. The case tested a rather exotic theory, the so-called migratory bird rule. Throughout the Upper Midwest and in the Dakotas, the receding glaciers of the Ice Age left "prairie potholes," lakes and wetlands with no connection to the sea. These waters were vital stopping-off points for migrating birds, and the corps maintained that this interstate travel connection gave it the authority to protect these ponds and wetlands from pollution or destruction. Rehnquist treated this theory as far-fetched. A federal law designed to protect the "navigable waters" of the United States could not be stretched to reach isolated ponds and wetlands, he said.

Rehnquist's opinion could be read in two ways. He had stressed the original language of the Clean Water Act, which referred to "navigable waters," a term that suggested it dealt only with rivers, lakes, and bays where boats could float. If so, the law did not reach wetlands far from major rivers. However, the ruling itself, as Rehnquist noted, dealt only with isolated waterways. For that reason, it did not help Rapanos, since, as the Sixth Circuit found, a "hydrological connection" existed between his land and Lake Huron, even though the connection was intermittent and by way of a drainage ditch.

Lawyers for the PLF filed a petition for certiorari on behalf of Ra-

---

2. 531 U.S. 159 (2002).

panos that argued the corps was still out of control and was violating both the Clean Water Act and the Constitution. While Congress had the power "to regulate commerce . . . among the several states," this power did not give the federal government the authority to regulate a farmer and his fields, the petition said. The appeal set forth a two-part legal argument: the Court should read the Clean Water Act strictly and narrowly; if not, the statute itself was unconstitutional because it exceeded Congress's power.

At issue was more than one hundred million acres of wetlands in the lower forty-eight states, said M. Reed Hopper, the PLF attorney for Rapanos, as well as the entire drainage basin for the Mississippi River. The corps claimed jurisdiction over these marshy lands and tens of thousands of tiny streams because they drained into the Mississippi or the Great Lakes. Hopper said that the law gave the federal government power over "navigable waters" and that it meant just what it said.

The Court had taken no action on Rapanos's petition in late June 2005 when a frail Chief Justice Rehnquist sounded the gavel for the summer recess. As the justices rose from their seats, O'Connor held Rehnquist's arm to steady him. A few days later, on July 1, O'Connor announced her plans to retire. And over the following Labor Day weekend, Rehnquist succumbed to cancer. In mid-July, President George W. Bush, to broad acclaim, had nominated John G. Roberts Jr. to fill O'Connor's seat. But less than forty-eight hours after Rehnquist's death, the president switched course and selected Roberts to replace Rehnquist. It was fitting, since Roberts had first came to Washington in 1980 to be a clerk for Rehnquist, at the time an associate justice.

When the gavel sounded again on the first Monday in October, Chief Justice Roberts was in the center seat. On Friday of that first week, the justices met for their regular closed-door conference to go over pending appeals, and they emerged with a surprise. The Court had granted the petition in *Rapanos v. United States* challenging the federal authority over wetlands.

Environmentalists were taken aback. The Clean Water Act and the Clean Air Act were the two most important antipollution measures in the nation's history. Congress had launched the environmental cleanup movement by giving federal regulators broad authority to stop pollution at its source. That broad federal jurisdiction had been affirmed for more than three decades by both Republican and Democratic administrations and by Congress under the control of both Republicans and Democrats. Roberts had been advertised as a conservative in the Rehnquist mold, but he also spoke to the Senate of the need for modesty and stability on the Court. He described himself as a believer in stare decisis, the doctrine that says the law should stand as decided. Yet in his first action as chief justice, the Roberts Court threatened to overturn thirty years of environmental law.

A second appeal from another Michigan developer was granted as well. June and Keith Carabell wanted to clear a piece of land near Lake St. Clair that included sixteen acres of wetlands. They said that an artificial berm surrounded the property and prevented water from flowing into the lake. Nonetheless, the Army Corps of Engineers refused to grant the permit because the land abutted a navigable waterway. Since this posed a different twist on the same issue, the Court agreed to hear *Carabell v. Army Corps* along with Rapanos.

Rapanos *and* Carabell

In essence, two questions were to be decided: Is there a legal limit on the federal authority over wetlands? And if so, how should it be defined?

Hopper was clear from his opening brief. He said the law gave federal authorities the power to prevent discharges of pollution into "navigable waters" and not much more. Leading the defense for the environment as well as for the federal government was, ironically enough, a Bush administration lawyer with solidly conservative credentials. U.S. Solicitor General Paul D. Clement was a forty-year-old Wisconsin native and a graduate of Harvard Law School. He had been an aide to Senator John Ashcroft (R-Mo.), had clerked for Judge Lawrence Silberman on the U.S. Court of Appeals in Washington, and then had clerked for Justice Scalia at the Supreme Court. In 2001, President Bush chose Clement as a chief deputy to Solicitor General Ted Olson, and when Olson stepped down, Clement replaced him.

By tradition, the solicitor general has a special, nonpartisan role. He represents the U.S. government, but he also advises the Court on the law. Environmental activists and the Bush administration were rarely in sync, but Clement's job, as he saw it, was to defend federal agencies and the laws passed by Congress, not to make policy for the Bush administration. He chose to argue the *Rapanos* and *Carabell* cases himself, and his briefs were unyielding. Congress did not exclude "non-navigable tributaries" from the reach of the Clean Water Act, he wrote, and had not done so for a very practical reason. If sewage, toxic chemicals, and medical waste can be dumped into these waterways, "the nation's largest rivers and lakes would be left highly vulnerable to degradation through upstream pollution discharges," he wrote (brief for United States, 21).

A final piece of the puzzle fell into place just before the oral argument on February 21, 2006. Bush had named Judge Samuel A. Alito Jr. to fill O'Connor's seat, and he won confirmation from the Senate in late January, when the Court was headed into its winter recess. February 21 was his first day on the bench.

The Oral Arguments

"This is a case of agency overreaching," Hopper began. "Contrary to the plain text of the [Clean Water] Act," the Army Corps of Engineers claims "jurisdiction over the entire tributary system, from the smallest trickle to the largest watershed, . . . sweeping in remote, nonnavigable wetlands twenty miles from the traditional navigable water."

Justice Scalia has never been a fan of the environmental laws, and his sympathies are almost never hidden during an oral argument. He usually plays the role of cheerleader for the lawyer on one side and attack dog for his opponent; he did not change strategies in *Rapanos.* "It goes somewhat beyond the smallest trickle, doesn't it?" Scalia offered in his role as Hopper's supporter. "Doesn't it also include ditches that currently don't have any trickle if they obtain a trickle during a rainstorm?"

Hopper was pleased to agree. They claim "the entire watershed," he said. The Mississippi River watershed stretches from the Appalachians in the east to the Rockies in the west. It "covers one million square miles," he said.

"So where would you put the line?" asked Justice Ruth Bader Ginsburg.

"I'd put the line where Congress put the line, Your Honor," he said. The law prohibits fill and dredge discharges "into the navigable waters."

"What about major tributaries?" Ginsburg continued.

Hopper hedged a bit. Congress "cannot regulate all tributaries," but it "could regulate some tributaries."

"Which ones?" Ginsburg asked.

It would depend "on a case-by-case basis," Hopper said. Ginsburg pressed further, and Hopper struggled to draw a clear line. "There's no clear indication that Congress intended to regulate any tributaries, let alone the entire tributary system," he said.

Hopper hedged because, in the past, the Supreme Court had said that the Clean Water Act covers more than navigable waters. In *United States v. Riverside Bayview Homes* (1985),[3] the justices unanimously upheld federal jurisdiction over wetlands that were adjacent to—and in a sense, a part of—a major lake or river.

In his first question, Alito highlighted the problem. "Does it make sense to say that any wetlands that abuts a traditionally navigable water is covered, but a tributary that leads right into a traditionally navigable water is not necessarily covered?" he asked.

Hopper could have suggested that the Court overrule *Riverside Bayview* and return to a strict focus on "navigable waters" only. Such a gambit would almost surely fail, since the Court rarely overturns its own precedents, particularly a unanimous ruling interpreting a statute. Hopper was forced to make the best of a bad situation. The 1985 ruling "makes sense," he said, because those wetlands were seen as "the equivalent of the navigable waterway."

From there, things got worse for Hopper. Justice David H. Souter attacked Hopper's entire theory of the case. The 1985 decision, Souter

---

3. 474 U.S. 121.

noted, was based on a "functional" view of the law. Hopper had several responses (none of them entirely convincing), and Souter continued his criticism. Hopper said that it would "raise significant constitutional questions" to permit federal regulation far upstream. The states could control this upstream pollution, he said. He also argued that determined polluters could be stopped if the government could find them and prove their pollution reached the Great Lakes.

JUSTICE SOUTER: Yes, but they're doing it for a functional reason. The functional reason is that if you put the poison in the adjacent wetland, it's going to get into the navigable water. Exactly the same argument can be made as you go further and further up the tributaries, and it seems to me that once you concede, as I think you have to, that there can be a regulation that goes beyond literally navigable water at the point at which the—the pollutant is added, then you have to follow the same logic right up through the watershed to—to any point at which a pollutant, once added, will eventually get into the navigable water.

MR. HOPPER: The reason that logic does not apply, Your Honor, is because the regulation of—of tributaries raises significant constitutional questions that are not implicated by the regulation of a wetland inseparably—

JUSTICE SOUTER: Then—then you have to accept the fact that—that Congress cannot effectively regulate the navigable—the—the condition of the navigable water itself because if all the—the—let's—let's assume there's a class of—of evil polluters out there who just want to wreck the—the navigable waters of the United States. All they have to do is get far enough upstream and they can dump anything they want to. It will eventually get into the navigable water, and Congress can't do anything about it on your theory.

Justice Souter pressed further.

JUSTICE SOUTER: In every case then, I mean, Congress would have to—I'm sorry—a scientist would have to analyze the molecules and—and trace them up, and so long as they could—could trace it to a specific discharge, they could get at it, but otherwise they couldn't? I mean, that—you know, you know what I'm getting at. That obviously would—would totally thwart the regulation.

MR. HOPPER: I don't—I don't believe it would, Your Honor. The—the—certainly Congress did not think so in section—

Even Scalia found that a bit much.

JUSTICE SCALIA: Well, I—couldn't you simply assume that anything that is discharged into a tributary ultimately goes where the tributary goes? Wouldn't it be enough to prove the discharge?

MR. HOPPER: Well, it certainly wasn't true in this case, Your Honor. The—

JUSTICE SCALIA: So you don't think it would be enough for the—for the government to prove the discharge into a tributary in order to prove that the act has been violated.

MR. HOPPER: No, Your Honor, I do not.

JUSTICE SCALIA: You really think it has to trace the molecules.

MR. HOPPER: Absolutely. That's—that's what the terms of the act require.

Chief Justice Roberts was still looking for a line to draw.

CHIEF JUSTICE ROBERTS: How do you—how do you define a tributary?

MR. HOPPER: Well, the—that's one of the problems here, Your Honor, is that—is that the agency has—has established a moving target for—for tributaries.

CHIEF JUSTICE ROBERTS: So what's your definition?

MR. HOPPER: Well, the—the definitions we're working with here, to which we object, is that—is that it includes anything in the hydrological connection.

The new chief justice has a mild manner, and he is patient with struggling advocates. He is also persistent, and he expects answers.

When he was an attorney before the Court, Roberts was renowned for his intense preparation. Before each of his arguments, he spent weeks devising questions and rehearsing answers. He was determined to be ready with the right answer, regardless of the question asked.

Hopper, however, apparently had decided that he was not going to answer Roberts's question. "I know what you object to, . . . but I don't know what test you would have us adopt for what constitutes a tributary," Roberts continued. "We're suggesting this Court need not define a tributary," Hopper said, "because under the Act all tributaries are excluded. The only—the only prohibited act—"

Roberts was not pleased. "Okay, we still don't know what you are excluding. I mean, the Missouri is a tributary of the Mississippi, but I assume it's still covered," he said. True, but that is "traditional navigable water," Hopper said. As the old saying goes, he had his story, and he was sticking to it.

Justice Kennedy leaned forward and threw Hopper a lifeline: "Well, it seems to me that what works in your favor is . . . *SWANCC?* I'm not quite sure how to pronounce the case," he said, referring to the acronym for the five-year-old ruling on "isolated" ponds and wetlands. "The migratory bird rule case where we said there had to be a significant nexus" between the wetland and navigable waters. Kennedy had joined Rehnquist's opinion in that case and cast a key vote for the 5-4 majority. If Hopper was going to win this case, he needed Kennedy's vote. "I think the Court is asking you to define a 'significant nexus,'" the justice told Hopper.

Hopper had used the term *significant nexus* in his brief, but he was not interested in defining it more precisely. It is not "standard for all waters," he told Kennedy. It applies only to "wetlands that are adjacent to traditional navigable waters," he said, referring back to the *Riverside Bayview* case. Kennedy obviously thought otherwise. He saw the notion of "significant nexus" as the key to the entire statute. Yet rather than adjust his argument to fit the justice's inquiry, Hopper dismissed it and stuck to his formulation of "navigable waters" and nothing more. A more adept lawyer might have used the opportunity to explain why no "significant nexus" existed between the Rapanos field and Lake Huron twenty miles away, but Hopper chose not to do so.

This exchange also revealed the disadvantage of having a lawyer from a national interest group. Hopper, from Sacramento, knew land-use law, and he understood the importance of winning a clear legal rule that would limit the reach of federal regulators. But he knew very little about the land near Saginaw and Midland, Michigan; the farm fields owned by Rapanos; or the drainage patterns. Whenever he was asked to describe the drainage ditch or the nearest tributary, he steered around the question or suggested that the relationship between the ditch and navigable water was not important.

MR. HOPPER: Let me also address something that this Court did in *SWANCC*. It was not the lack of a hydrological connection in that case that informed this Court's decision to exclude those isolated ponds from federal jurisdiction. It was the fact that those—that the regulation of those isolated ponds did not meet the terms of the act and there was no clear indication Congress intended to regulate isolated ponds. I submit that's this case. In this case, there is no clear indication that Congress intended to regulate wetlands twenty miles from the nearest navigable water.

JUSTICE GINSBURG: We're told that one of them was much closer.

MR. HOPPER: The—the record is silent as to the distance between—

JUSTICE GINSBURG: What about the Pine River? Are you—that's not twenty miles away, is it?

MR. HOPPER: We don't know how far that is because the record is silent as to the distance between those water bodies.

JUSTICE GINSBURG: Do you know? The—the solicitor general represented to us that it was very close. Are you disputing that as a matter of fact?

MR. HOPPER: I don't know what he means by very close. The—the solicitor general would agree with me that—that there's nothing in the record to indicate what those distances are. And it's irrelevant in—in our opinion, whether it's—whether it's a mile or twenty miles or fifty miles or one hundred miles, and that's the point. There does—under the—under the federal regulations, a true, significant nexus is not required, just any hydrological connection. This is a presumption on congressional authority.

> This expansive interpretation destroys any distinction between what is national and what is local under—as—as has already been pointed out. Under the federal regulations, you can't dig a ditch in this country without federal approval. You can't fill it in. You can't clean it out without federal approval. This reads the term navigable right out of the statute. We—we ask this Court not to allow these agencies—

When he took his seat, he had left the Court with a stark choice, and he offered little help to the conservatives who wanted to limit the authority of the corps.

Timothy A. Stoepker, a lawyer from Detroit, took the lectern next to argue the Carabells' appeal. His clients looked to have a stronger case than Rapanos because a ditch and a berm prevented the marshy areas from draining into the lake. "The record is very clear," Stoepker began. The Carabells' "wetland is hydrologically isolated from any navigable water of the United States." So "water never ran off of this land," Scalia commented. "And the only reason it's water of the United States is that there are some puddles on this land. Right? And if there were no puddles, it wouldn't be a water of the U.S. It would just be land of the U.S." Scalia said again to emphasize the point for his colleagues. But several minutes earlier, Justice Kennedy had raised a problem. "Was it also clear that after the improvement, there would be no drainage?" he asked. "After the improvement, there could be drainage," Stoepker replied. It seemed to take a few minutes for that answer to sink in.

Justice John Paul Stevens, who had turned eighty-six the preceding spring, often sits quietly through much of the argument, like a wise old owl intently watching the proceedings. Lawyers often say the question they most fear during an oral argument is a soft-spoken, kindly inquiry from Stevens. Sometimes it begins with, "Counsel, may I inquire about one point that has confused me to this point?"

Scalia was in the midst of arguing Stoepker's case for him when Stevens spoke up. "I'm still puzzled by your answer to Justice Kennedy," he said, his words broken by joking comments by Scalia. "What if there's no hydrological connection today, but there would be after you built your project?" he asked. "Would that be a sufficient reason to deny a permit?" No, Stoepker said. "The test is from the outset, Your Honor." The "resulting impact" does not give the corps jurisdiction to stop the project at its inception, he said. "But isn't it sort of foolish to say that we're concerned about pollution, but only if you catch it in advance?" Stevens continued. "That doesn't make sense."

Suddenly, a new image was before the Court. The Detroit lawyer began with the image of an isolated wooded area with "some puddles" on it, as Scalia put it. Kennedy and Stevens conjured up a different site: a shopping center with an asphalt parking lot that sends rainwater gushing down the drains and into the lake. Maybe there was a "hydrological connection" and there would be a real impact on Lake St. Clair after all if the Carabells were free to develop their land.

Now, it was the turn of the U.S. solicitor general. Clement sought to persuade the Court that there were no limits on the federal government's power to prevent pollution of the nation's waters, even if that meant regulating wetlands, streams, or ditches located miles from a navigable lake. But no government lawyer would want to say the government's power is essentially unlimited, particularly when he is standing before the justices of the Supreme Court. That position would surely goad them in adopting a strict limit. The better course was to argue that the *Rapanos* and *Carabell* cases involved at most a minor twist on a settled matter. Not surprisingly, Clement chose that course.

"In *United States v. Riverside Bayview Homes,* this Court unanimously upheld the corps's jurisdiction over wetlands that were not themselves navigable," Clement began. These wetlands were described as "adjacent to" navigable waters, he said. "The principal difference between the *Rapanos* wetlands and the wetlands at issue in *Riverside Bayview* are [*sic*] that the *Rapanos* wetlands are adjacent to a nonnavigable tributary," he said.

Just as in horseshoes, where close counts, Clement was arguing that the Court had already accepted the principle that close counts where water is concerned. Water seeps under the ground, and after heavy rains it can top a barrier and flow to the nearest waterway. The wetlands in the *Riverside Bayview* case were close to navigable waters, and the *Rapanos* wetlands were close to a tributary of a navigable waterway, he argued.

But Roberts and Scalia were not buying the idea. They saw a big difference between a drainage ditch and a navigable river. Clement had completed only two sentences when Chief Justice Roberts and Justice Scalia interrupted.

CHIEF JUSTICE ROBERTS: How do you define *tributary*?

MR. CLEMENT: Mr. Chief—

CHIEF JUSTICE ROBERTS: The tributary—you say they're adjacent to a nonnavigable tributary. That's a—a culvert, a ditch. Right?

MR. CLEMENT: Well, not in all these cases, Mr. Chief Justice.

CHIEF JUSTICE ROBERTS: But in the *Rapanos* case.

MR. CLEMENT: No, not—not—that's actually not true. There are three specific wetlands that are at issue in the *Rapanos* case. One of those, the Pine River site, as its name suggests, is adjacent to the Pine River, which is a body of water that has water flowing through it all year round. It's a river. I don't think anybody would look at that and say that's not a tributary of the downstream navigable rivers. And I think that's why, in fairness—

CHIEF JUSTICE ROBERTS: What about—what about the other—the other sites?

MR. CLEMENT: The—the other sites are—are adjacent to man-made ditches that also drain in. If I just—can I just say, though, I think the fact that the Pine River site is so obviously a tributary under—under any definition is one of the reasons, along with the theory that you heard advanced by petitioners, that this case—

CHIEF JUSTICE ROBERTS: But your argument assumes that the ditches that go to the other two sites are also tributaries.

MR. CLEMENT: Absolutely, Mr. Chief Justice. I just want to make the point that this case, because of the theory petitioners have advanced, has not really unearthed or focused on the definition of a tributary, but let me get to it because the corps has defined the definition of a tributary. And the definition of a tributary is basically any channelized body of water that takes water in a flow down to the traditional navigable water—

JUSTICE SCALIA: Even when it's not a body of water.

MR. CLEMENT: Even—

JUSTICE SCALIA: A storm drain, even—even when it's not filled with water, is a tributary. Right?

MR. CLEMENT: Justice Scalia, absolutely.

JUSTICE SCALIA: Okay.

MR. CLEMENT: The corps has not drawn a distinction between man-made channels or ditches and natural channels or ditches. And, of course, it would be very absurd for the corps to do that since the Erie Canal is a ditch.

JUSTICE SCALIA: I suggest it's very absurd to call that waters of the United States. It's a drainage ditch dug—you know, dug by the municipality or—you know, or a gutter in a street. To call that waters of the United States seems to me extravagant.

MR. CLEMENT: Well, let me say two things, Justice Scalia. First of all, this case has not been litigated under the theory that the key difference is whether it's man-made or natural, and that defines somehow the scope of a tributary. And I think there's a good reason for that, which is the second point, which is as the corps experts—from the experts, the corps will tell you the process of making the natural rivers navigable has all been about the process of channelizing them and creating man-made, artificial channels in them to the point where the difference between that which is a man-made channel and that which is a natural channel is both difficult to discern and utterly beside the point for purposes of this regulatory scheme.

JUSTICE SCALIA: What—what percentage of the—of the territory of the United States do you believe is—is subjected to permits from the Corps of Engineers on your theory whenever you want to move dirt, whenever you want to deposit sand? What—what percentage of the total land mass of the United States, if you define tributary as broadly as you define it to include? Every storm drain? I mean, it's the whole country, isn't it?

Scalia was not going easy on his former law clerk.

Clement was not going to win over Scalia or apparently Roberts. Like Scalia, the chief justice thought the law—and indeed the Constitution—required a limit on the federal authority. "At some point, you've got to say, 'Stop,'" he told Clement.

While Souter's "evil polluters" question had exposed the problem with Hopper's strict focus on navigable waters, Scalia's jabs exposed the difficulty Clement faced. If the possibility of one drop of water flowing downstream were enough to give the Corps of Engineers jurisdiction, its reach could encompass the "total land mass" of the country, as Scalia had put it.

Both sides could count their votes by this point in the argument. Souter, Stevens, and Ginsburg would uphold the government's authority in this case, and so too, in all likelihood, would Justice Stephen G. Breyer, who had been uncharacteristically silent so far. The four of them had regularly voted to uphold federal regulatory power, and they were not likely to reverse course when environmental protection was at stake.

Scalia and Roberts rejected the government's position, and so too would a characteristically silent Justice Clarence Thomas. The decision then would turn on the veteran Kennedy or the newcomer Alito. Both had roots in the Reagan administration. Kennedy was Reagan's third and final appointee and had joined regularly with Rehnquist to limit federal authority. Alito was a lawyer in Reagan's Justice Department, but he had much less of a record on the issue of federal power.

Earlier in the hour, Kennedy had said that the *SWANCC* case was the key precedent, and it spoke of wetlands that have a "significant nexus" with navigable waters. But Hopper whiffed when Kennedy asked him to explain why there was no significant nexus, or connection, between the Rapanos fields and Lake Huron.

Amid the barrage of questions from Scalia and Roberts, Kennedy intervened to raise the *SWANCC* case with Clement. "It seems to me that you have to show that there's some significant relation between the wetlands you're regulating, or seeking to regulate, and the navigable water." "I agree with that, Justice Kennedy," Clement replied. "That's seemed to me so far to have been missing from the discussion," Kennedy said. Clement saw the opportunity and took it. He explained at some length that Corps of Engineers basically follows that approach because pollution upstream affects the waters downstream. "You can start with the 'significant nexus' test and see it's been met," he said. "Is there a significant nexus between the tributaries and the navigable waters in which they flow into? And I think the answer is yes." He went on to explain how the environmental regulators would see a "significant nexus between wetlands that are adjacent to waters otherwise within the Corps jurisdiction." The Court's *Riverside Bayview* decision had already blessed that approach, he said. "I think 'significant nexus' is precisely the kind of test you'd want the corps" to follow, he concluded.

No sooner had he finished than Roberts and Scalia went back on the attack. The chief justice accused Clement of adopting the "one drop a year" test. If one drop of water could flow from an interior wetland to the sea, the Corps of Engineers would have jurisdiction over it, Roberts said. Clement agreed, at least in theory. "But if there's one drop, grant the permit," he interjected. This was a small but important point. The corps was arguing that it had the authority to require a permit before a wetland was filled in. But in many—probably most—cases, it would grant the permit and allow the developer to proceed.

Unlike Hopper, Clement described the water flow from the fields owned by Rapanos. He drew a closer link to navigable waters than was suggested by Scalia's talk of "puddles" and drainage ditches. "The Pine River site, as its name suggests, is adjacent to the Pine River," Clement said. "It's a river . . . that has water flowing through it all year round."

Clement finished on a strong note. To rule for Rapanos would give polluters a "free dump zone" in streams and wetlands that were not navigable, he said. And state regulators could not be expected to fill the void if the federal authority were stripped away, he added. His argument stressed that this case involved not just wetlands but also the federal government's role in preventing water pollution. If the Clean Water Act was just about "navigable waters," then federal regulators could not prevent pollution of streams and tributaries across the nation.

"I think it's a bit much to ask a legislator in Wisconsin or Minnesota to stop local development in order to protect the water quality and flood control propensities of the Mississippi River in Mississippi,"

Clement said. "That's why it was manifest in 1972 that there was a need for a federal solution to this problem. That federal solution includes as two of its most important components, first, getting at water pollution at its source . . . and secondly, covering the tributary system without which the navigable waters will continue to be polluted." With that, Clement took his seat.

When the justices left the bench, it was clear that they would be closely divided, although it was not clear which side would win. The decision came on June 19, 2006, and it was still not entirely clear who had won. The Court split 4-1-4. Justice Scalia "announced the judgment" of the Court, but his opinion spoke for only a plurality of four. Indeed, it takes at least five votes (or a majority of nine justices) to set good law. As such, when a majority cannot be reached, only a judgment is announced, and it lacks the weight of precedent. Scalia said that the Clean Water Act reaches only "permanent, standing or continuously flowing bodies of water," not wetlands that are connected by streams or channels which flow "occasionally or intermittently." He did not go as far as Hopper to say the law covers only "navigable waters." Nonetheless, Scalia's opinion would have ended federal jurisdiction over most wetlands in the interior of the United States, including nearly all those in the West, where stream beds are dry for much of the year. Chief Justice Roberts and Justices Thomas and Alito signed Scalia's opinion.

In dissent, Justice Stevens took Scalia to task for judicial action. In the past, the Court's rulings upholding federal protection for wetlands were "faithful to our duty to respect the work product of the legislative and executive branches of our government. Today's judicial amendment of the Clean Water Act is not," he said.[4] Justices Souter, Ginsburg, and Breyer joined Stevens's opinion.

Justice Kennedy wrote a solo opinion. No other justice joined it, and he did not join either the Scalia or Stevens opinion. But since it provided the fifth vote, Kennedy's view was decisive. He described Scalia's opinion as "inconsistent with the text, structure and purpose" of the Clean Water Act and further described the opinion as "unduly dismissive" of

4. 547 U.S. 715, 788 (2006).

the importance of wetlands to the rivers and lakes downstream. Kennedy also noted that Congress had described rock, sand, and dirt as pollutants that could wash downstream, and the Corps of Engineers could decide—certainly better than a group of judges—whether the runoff from a filled wetland could affect downstream. A native of California, Kennedy certainly understood that dry creek beds can send "torrents thundering" downstream in the winter, as he put it. Scalia's opinion would have excluded all these channels because they were not "continuous flowing" bodies of water.[5]

Kennedy voted to overturn the Sixth Circuit's decision because its opinion had not applied the "significant nexus" test. Since he joined Scalia's foursome on this point, it meant Rapanos had won on a 5-4 vote. But in substance, Kennedy said that his view of the law was much closer to the government's and to the Stevens dissent than to Scalia's opinion. And because his opinion provided the fifth vote, lower courts would follow his analysis. The government can protect wetlands that are well inland as long as the Corps of Engineers can show that filling them will have an impact downstream, he said. "Thus, the end result in these cases and many others to be considered by the Corps may be the same as that suggested by [Stevens], namely, that the corps's assertion of jurisdiction is valid," Kennedy concluded.[6]

It may have ended in a photo finish, but the federal protection for the nation's wetlands had prevailed in its greatest test in the Supreme Court.

---

5. 547 U.S. 715, 769 (2006).

6. 547 U.S. 715, 783 (2006).

Randall v. Sorrell

Arguing over Campaign Finance in Vermont

ARGUED FEBRUARY 28, 2006

BRENT KENDALL

In 1997, Vermont passed a campaign finance law, Act 64, that imposed strict limits both on expenditures by candidates for office during the election cycle and on the contributions of individuals, political groups, and parties. Neil Randall, a state legislator, sued Vermont attorney general William Sorrell, arguing that the limits unconstitutionally infringed on First Amendment freedom of speech. In Randall's view, the Supreme Court had declared all expenditure limits unconstitutional in Buckley v. Valeo (1976), and Act 64's contribution limits were unconstitutionally low. The district court struck down the expenditure limits but upheld most of the contribution limits. Only contribution limits on political parties—under which national, state, and local parties together could give only four hundred dollars to a statewide candidate—were unconstitutionally low. Both parties appealed the ruling to the U.S. Court of Appeals for the Second Circuit. The circuit court reversed, ruling that all of Vermont's contribution limits were constitutional. The Second Circuit also found that the expenditure limits would be constitutional as long as they were "narrowly tailored" to the state's interests.

To listen to passages from oral arguments indicated with 🔊, visit www.goodquarrel.com.

WHEN VERMONT'S LEGISLATORS PASSED A CONTROVERSIAL 1997 law that brought sweeping reforms to the state's campaign finance system, they knew they were testing some long-standing legal boundaries. Not only was the state planning to place very strict limits on the amount of money that citizens and political parties could donate to candidates running for office, Vermont also wanted to limit the amount of money candidates could spend on their campaigns, a proposal that ran headlong into the U.S. Supreme Court's thirty-year-old landmark ruling in *Buckley v. Valeo,*[1] which struck down campaign spending limits as an unconstitutional restriction on speech.

The law's backers, however, said that the current political landscape bore little resemblance to that of the *Buckley* era. The costs of mounting effective political campaigns had skyrocketed. Well-funded special interests were ever more influential in the legislative process. Nothing less than the public's faith in government was at stake.

The reforms, lawmakers said, were necessary to prevent real and perceived corruption and to remove the incessant time demands of unlimited fund-raising so that legislators could refocus their attention where it belonged: on running the government.

Future presidential candidate Howard Dean, Vermont's governor at the time, enthusiastically signed the reforms into law. "Money does buy access, and we're kidding ourselves and Vermonters if we deny it," Dean said in his 1997 inaugural address, a speech that helped prompt the reforms. The Second Circuit's opinion in this case even quoted Dean's remark.[2]

Vermont's position as the vanguard of the campaign-finance reform movement was unusual, to say the least, given that the state was one of the cheapest in which to run for office. The state ranked forty-ninth in spending for gubernatorial campaigns. Its statewide population was smaller than that of a single State Senate district in California. Television and newspaper advertising came at bargain prices. Consequently, Vermont set its spending and contribution limits at levels that would be unthinkably low in other states.

---

1. 424 U.S. 1 (1976).

2. 382 F.3d 91, 2nd Cir. (2004).

Candidates for governor could spend no more than three hundred thousand dollars on their campaigns. The limits decreased steadily for down-ticket political races, bottoming out at four thousand dollars and two thousand dollars for State Senate and State House contests, respectively, sums small enough that the average Vermonter could sell a beat-up used car and finance his or her entire campaign without worrying about being outspent by candidates with bigger war chests.

As for the state's new contribution limits, candidates for statewide office could accept no more than four hundred dollars from a single donor or political committee. The same caps even applied to contributions that candidates received from their political parties. Again, the limits were even lower for down-ticket races. A candidate for state representative or a local office could accept no individual contribution larger than two hundred dollars. The law's supporters said Vermont's low contribution limits—the lowest in the nation—weeded out only "suspiciously large" donations.

As expected, the law faced an immediate legal challenge, and in 2000, a federal judge struck down Vermont's spending limits and a portion of its contribution limits. In 2004, however, the federal appeals court in New York reversed much of the trial judge's ruling and handed down a decision favorable to Vermont. A three-judge panel of the Second Circuit Court of Appeals then ruled unanimously that the state's contribution limits were constitutional. On the closely watched question of spending limits, the panel was divided, deciding 2-1 that the caps might pass constitutional muster in spite of the Supreme Court's contrary *Buckley* decision. *Buckley,* the appeals court said, was not an absolute bar to spending limits. Instead, Vermont could save its spending caps if it could prove that they were narrowly tailored and that no less-restrictive alternative was available.

From the day the Second Circuit's ruling came down, the Vermont case seemed a good candidate for Supreme Court review, especially after the state joined its opponents in urging the high court to take up the case, an unusual and aggressive strategy for a party that had prevailed at the appeals court level. However, Vermont, along with the interest groups that intervened to help defend the state's law, wanted clarity. A green light from the Supreme Court could inspire other states to enact campaign finance reforms, a prospect confirmed by eighteen states that submitted an amicus curiae (friend of the court) brief supporting Vermont's position.

When the high court announced that it would indeed consider the case, most observers believed that Vermont faced an uphill battle in winning over a majority of the justices.[3] The state's attorney general, William H. Sorrell, who would be making his first Supreme Court appearance to defend the law, said as much in one of the local papers: "We are admittedly swimming upstream because the Vermont law flies in the face of a 1968 court ruling" (Remsen 2006).

Though the outcome of the case was not likely to hinge on Sorrell's performance at the oral argument—numerous other factors came into play, including the quality of the written legal briefs and the justices' predispositions on the issue—a slam-dunk presentation from the attorney general certainly would help the state's cause.

For twenty minutes, Sorrell would have a face-to-face chance to persuade any justices who might be sitting on the fence. Unfortunately for Vermont, Sorrell's appearance before the Court proved rocky. When the state's attorney general took to the podium on a late February morning to make his case, it took all of three minutes to see that a slam dunk was not in the offing, thanks to an unrelenting line of tough questions from Chief Justice John G. Roberts Jr., the Court's confident new leader, who had been on the job for just five months. Off balance from the start, Sorrell never fully recovered, as other justices picked up where Roberts left off.

The grilling Sorrell received in the crowded courtroom was especially striking because the first half hour of the argument proceeded sleepily. Sorrell's opponent, conservative Indiana lawyer James Bopp Jr., was up first, with the easier task of arguing against the Vermont law. Representing a group of challengers that included a sitting legislator, aspiring political candidates, the state Republican committee, and an antiabortion organization, Bopp was arguing his fourth case before the Court, a privilege he won literally by chance. Both he and a local Vermont lawyer on the case wanted to argue; they settled the matter with a coin flip, which Bopp won (Bopp, interview by author; Remsen 2006).

3. 548 U.S. 230 (2006).

When Bopp rose to address the bench, he articulated a clear and straightforward message: the Constitution could not tolerate Vermont's law because it restricted the core political speech the First Amendment had been designed to protect. As Bopp began his argument, he made point after point without any interruption from the Court: "This Court has never allowed the government to prohibit candidates from communicating relevant information to voters during an election." Vermont's law, he said, is incompatible with any reasonable interpretation of the First Amendment." When a candidate has spent all the money allowed by Vermont, he or she "may not drive to the village green to address a rally, may not return the phone call from a reporter at the local newspaper, and may not call a neighbor to urge her to get out to vote."

Bopp talked for three full minutes before a justice jumped in with a question. In his previous appearances, Bopp had never received so much room to make his initial arguments. Justice Ruth Bader Ginsburg broke in first. After asking for clarification on a procedural point, Ginsburg asked Bopp if he was arguing that spending limits on candidates could never be justified. Well, Bopp said, the Court had considered "a dozen times" in which the government sought to limit spending, and "despite the work of the most brilliant lawyers in the United States," no one had come up with a compelling governmental interest that legally justified the restrictions.

Justice Antonin G. Scalia, who, based on his positions in earlier cases, was a clear Bopp ally, jumped in a short time later not with a question but to give Bopp an assist. Instead of reducing the time candidates spend raising funds, Scalia said, Vermont's law did the opposite. The state's low limits on the size of donations meant that candidates would have to find a larger pool of contributors. "You make a big point of this in your brief, as I recall," Scalia suggested. "It's rather like the murderer asking for mercy because he's an orphan, having killed his parents," he said. Bopp agreed. "It is a self-justifying statute by imposing the lowest contribution limits in—in the nation, adjusted for inflation for 1974 dollars, when the thousand-dollar limit was approved. This is a contribution limit of fifty dollars for an—"

Justice Anthony Kennedy interrupted, seemingly ready to pressure

Bopp with a rather difficult question: "Well, to get back to Justice [David H.] Souter's questions, could you answer it this way? Let's assume that some members of the Court simply accepted the proposition that money buys access. And—and I don't think maybe we can take judicial notice of that, but I—I think that's a common-sense conclusion that we can reach. And you tend to fight this in your brief to say that this doesn't happen. I tend to doubt that. I tend to think money does buy access. What—if—if we or I were to conclude that, what would follow?" Bopp twice started a response, but Kennedy interrupted. And suddenly, the question wasn't so tough at all, because Kennedy was going to give Bopp the right answer: "I mean, isn't the answer that this is up to the voters?" Kennedy asked rhetorically. "The voters can see what's going on and throw the legislator out if they choose." "Indeed," Bopp said, and once again he was on track.

Bopp's appearance lacked much intensity or suspense, as he was pushed by justices only occasionally, a bad early sign for Vermont. He proceeded matter-of-factly, at times with the tone of a man having a leisurely conversation on his front porch. Only once did Bopp go too far out on a limb and get criticized for it. Vermont, Bopp said, "could not identify one single politician . . . that anyone would claim was corrupted in any way by a contribution. . . . They could not name one single incumbent politician in Vermont that neglected any specific duty that he or she had." Ironically, it was Scalia who couldn't let Bopp's remark pass without comment. "You expect them to name names?" the justice asked with a laugh. "I mean, really, that's a lot to ask."

During Bopp's thirty minutes, he and the justices danced back and forth on one question. The Court wanted to know when, if ever, a state would be within its rights to enact Vermont-like restrictions on campaigning. Bopp was hard to pin down. He avoided taking the absolute position that such restrictions could never be warranted. Instead, he tried to keep things focused on the case at hand. "These are real limits on people in Vermont," Bopp said. "And it seems to me that to approve the lowest contribution limits in the nation and these very low expenditure limits, the state would have to demonstrate that Vermont is the most corrupt state in the nation. And they're far from it."

The pace and energy of the argument changed quickly when Sorrell rose to address the Court. While the justices gave Bopp three minutes of uninterrupted time to begin his argument, Sorrell received all of twenty-two seconds, time for just four sentences. Instead of proceeding with a prepared opening, the Vermont attorney general attempted to rekindle a dialogue on Justice Kennedy's earlier proposition that money does buy access. "It clearly does," Sorrell said. But more than that, he said, testimony at trial indicated that "on the bad days, it buys influence."

Roberts, however, interrupted and initiated one of the most memorable exchanges from his first year on the high court, an interrogation that ultimately forced Sorrell to concede that his legal team had overstated a key argument it made in the written briefs. "Counsel, you say in your brief . . . that the record convincingly shows that the ties among donor groups and elected officials often *determine* the positions officials take," Roberts said. "Can you give me an example of an official who took a position because of the ties to donor groups?" The president of the Senate, Sorrell said, had refused to sign one piece of legislation because he did not want to lose campaign donations from food manufacturers.

JUSTICE ROBERTS: So your position is that that official's official positions were determined by the donor groups, as you say in your brief?

MR. SORRELL: Influenced and—

JUSTICE ROBERTS: Well, your brief says *determined.*

MR. SORRELL: Have an influence, and we would suggest an undue influence in some cases.

JUSTICE ROBERTS: So it should say *influenced* rather than *determined?*

MR. SORRELL: We didn't have anyone, as Justice Scalia asked, who stood up and admitted to having taken bribes.

Roberts, one of the best Supreme Court attorneys of his generation before he joined the judiciary, was not done chipping away at Sorrell's case. "How many prosecutions for political corruption have you brought?" he asked a moment later. None, Sorrell said, that he was aware of.

JUSTICE ROBERTS: Would you describe your state as a clean state politically or as a corrupt one?

MR. SORRELL: We have a real problem in Vermont. In over sixty-five hearings before our legislature and then through a ten-day trial, we established that, as the trial court said, the threat of corruption in Vermont is far from illusory.

JUSTICE SCALIA: To the extent that Vermont legislators can be bought off by fifty-one dollars? That's very sad.

Amid the courtroom laughter, Sorrell was reeling and confused. Scalia had taken Vermont's contribution limits and, adjusting for inflation, translated them into 1976 dollars, the year *Buckley* upheld contribution limits of one thousand dollars. The creative math, however, should not have come as a total surprise to Sorrell. Scalia almost certainly took his cue from the other side's legal brief, which offered the mathematical translation in a footnote. Justice Stephen G. Breyer, a member of the Court's liberal wing who frequently jousts with the conservative Scalia on the bench, explained to Sorrell what his colleague had done. "He sometimes thinks in the past," Breyer said with a smile, triggering another round of laughter.

Sorrell attempted to turn the focus back to why Vermont's contribution limits were inadequate. Even one of the law's challengers, Sorrell said, admitted that "if you receive a one-thousand-dollar contribution in Vermont, this is one of the petitioners, then Vermonters think that you've been bought." Roberts quickly reinserted himself: "And presumably they act accordingly at the polls," he said. "If they think someone has been bought, I assume they don't reelect the person."

Five minutes in, Sorrell had done nothing but play defense. Instead of attempting a direct answer to Roberts, he tried to shift gears and return to one of his big-picture themes: that modern-day campaigns were different from the old *Buckley* days, when the Supreme Court thought that limits on campaign spending were not needed.

But a moment later, Breyer, who promised to be a key vote in the case, interrupted to offer some of his concerns, particularly that the law would put political challengers at a "tremendous disadvantage" against incumbents.

> I and my friends have the following thought: we don't know who the candidates for state rep are, but we want a Republican slate, or we want a Democratic slate. So we get all our five dollars together, give them to the Democratic Party or the Republican Party in Vermont, and lo and behold, that party cannot give more than a hundred dollars in an election to a state rep etc. Now, to the ear, that sounds as if a challenger or a slate of challengers or a party that wants to challenge is going to have a really tough time. So I want you to explain it.

Sorrell disagreed. Vermont had established at trial, he said, that even under the new limits, "candidates can amass the resources necessary to run effective campaigns at all levels."

During these exchanges, Justice Breyer for the first time brought up the name of Ralph K. Winter, the dissenting Second Circuit judge who had blasted Vermont's spending limits as a well-meaning but deeply misguided assault on liberty. Weighing in at more than one hundred pages, Winter's dissent provided a powerful guide on how to criticize the law. Anyone looking to predict the toughest questions Sorrell would face at the Supreme Court needed only to look to Winter's opinion.

Winter saw Vermont's restrictions as heavily slanted toward incumbents, and he was particularly troubled that the limits applied over an entire two-year election cycle, meaning that candidates who faced contested primaries were subject to the same limits as those running unopposed within their parties. The candidates with the toughest fights would have to make their money go twice as far. And incumbents did not usually face tough primaries. Winter also offered strong criticism of the state's statistical reliance on average spending in past elections as a guide for where to set the new legal limits. "It's the non-average election," Winter wrote, "that is often the historic election, one in which the outcome is heavily contested, the debate is most widespread, the public interest is at its highest, and the most money is spent."[4]

The justices picked up on all of Winter's criticisms, mentioning Winter by name on four occasions. Despite his awareness of Winter's concerns, Sorrell did not always seem armed with effective rebuttals when

4. 382 F.3d 91, at 239 (Winter dissenting).

the high court echoed those points. Sorrell's oral presentation relied heavily on Vermont's data for average campaign spending, and the justices repeatedly criticized this approach.

MR. SORRELL: The reality is that in virtually all classes of races . . . average spending was below these expenditure limits, and these include contested cases with primaries [and] without.

JUSTICE SCALIA: That's just what I said. Your figures show that the average spending is below, but that's not what's significant. What's significant is what Justice Breyer posed, where there is a contested race and some new candidate wants to unseat somebody who's been in there for years. That's where the shoe pinches.

Sorrell said that Vermont had taken that circumstance into account and had decided to subject incumbents to lower spending limits than challengers. Although some outlier races might occur, Sorrell said, "we have core constitutional interests in trying to enhance the integrity of our campaigns. We have this problem. The legislature reached a balance here."

Sorrell later pointed out that one of the Vermont political candidates challenging the law, Donald Brunelle, had admitted to having run a competitive House race for one thousand dollars. When Scalia asked if Brunelle had had a primary, Sorrell did not know the answer. (Brunelle did not.) "That's another feature of this scheme that I find quite puzzling," Scalia said. "You get the same expenditure limit for the election cycle whether you go through a primary or not. What an advantage that is for the incumbent."

Sorrell said that Vermont's primaries differed from those in most states by taking place just eight weeks before the general election.

> There was testimony in the record that those who have a primary might actually get a bump over others who are not challenged. But as the district court pointed out, in Vermont what makes Vermont different is that our primary is late. It's the second Tuesday in September, and so it's less than eight weeks from the general election. It's not like having a primary in the spring.
>
> And as the legislature during those sixty-five hearings considered the cam-

> paigning, they considered all kinds of campaigns, including contested primaries and not, and again, average spending in these campaigns was, with minor exception of the single-member Senate districts, of which there are three—that average spending was below these expenditure limits. So in the average campaign, you could actually spend more than—than on average is being spent.
>
> And the issue, when you've got competing constitutional interests, is whether we address our problems of corruption, appearance of corruption. We try to free up candidates' and public officials' time from fund-raising. We try to create competitive elections and bring more citizens into the process, voting, grassroots campaigning, and standing for election. We want more people to run.

Justice Souter wanted to know how many of the political races Vermont used to calculate average spending were campaigns that included contested primaries. Sorrell said he did not know, but he did know that his experts took data from all races and came up with a figure for average spending.

Unfortunately for Sorrell, many members of the high court seemed to share Winter's view that Vermont's averages were not worth much. If, Souter said, a political challenger is "lucky enough to win [the primary], he's going to get to the general election and he's going to be broke. That's the problem that we're concerned with."

The argument drifted into more technical areas of the law, but as his time was winding down, Sorrell made one last attempt to score some broad and forceful points: "So Justice [Louis D.] Brandeis said that there's room under our system for a courageous State to experiment—" But Justice Breyer interrupted to ask a technical question about whether a meet-and-greet with voters over coffee and donuts counted toward a candidate's spending caps. By the time Sorrell finished answering, his moment on the nation's biggest legal stage was over.

Unlike Bopp, Sorrell didn't have the luxury of thirty minutes to argue his case. The final ten minutes of Vermont's argument time was allotted to Brenda Wright of the National Voting Rights Institute, who was representing the voters and interest groups that had intervened to defend the law. Wright produced some solid answers, but the Court met her with skepticism, too. She began by addressing Kennedy and Roberts's argument that voters should just vote crooked politicians out of office. The public, she said, does not always see the corruption. "It's important to point out that some of the most serious examples of corruption on this record . . . were not examples that ever became public except in the course of the trial of this case when we had witnesses come forward to testify," Wright said. But, Scalia responded, campaign donations are made in public view. And if voters think those donations taint their politicians, citizens will logically vote those people out of office. The problem, Wright said, is that in an unlimited spending system, all the candidates accept as much cash as they can and tell the public that they have no choice but to do so. But, Roberts said, "Vermont would be the last place that you'd be worried about it." It's cheap and easy to go door-to-door, "and that's what the Vermonters expect." Vermont and its supporters, Roberts said, had "a real dilemma" in justifying the state's campaign finance law. On the one hand, the state was arguing that candidates did not need a lot of money to run effectively; on the other, the state was suggesting that the state was facing a serious problem with too much money. "Which is it?" he asked.

As the session wound down, Breyer refocused the argument on the Court's landmark decision in *Buckley:* "Am I not bound by that? . . . I'd like to hear why you think I'm not bound by a past precedent in an important matter, with which I may or may not have agreed at the time." Wright argued that the Court did not have to overrule *Buckley* to side with Vermont because the ruling did not dictate that all future spending limits were invalid. And, she said, Vermont had a number of weighty governmental interests that justified its actions.

In the end, neither Wright's nor Sorrell's arguments gained much traction inside the marble palace. Vermont's big test case ended with a whimper.

Justice Breyer announced the Court's 6-3 decision striking down the Vermont law four months later. He was the only justice in the Court's four-member liberal wing to vote against the state. Breyer disposed of the law's spending limits with relative ease, saying that the Court found no special justification for overruling the thirty years of *Buckley* precedent. Vermont and its supporters, he wrote in the Court's principal opinion, "have not shown, for example, any dramatic increase in corruption or its appearance in Vermont; nor have they shown that expenditure limits are the only way to attack that problem."[5]

Breyer devoted more of the opinion to explaining why the state's contribution limits were also invalid. Though the Court had upheld previous restrictions on campaign contributions, "we must recognize the existence of some lower bound," he wrote. "At some point the constitutional risks to the democratic electoral process become too great."[6] Among the reasons he cited for invalidating the contribution limits, Breyer cited the very low dollar limits, the potential negative effect on challengers, and the adverse impact on political parties.

Vermont's loss was total: the ruling marked the first time the Court had ever invalidated a contribution limit.

5. 548 U.S. 230, 243 (2006).

6. 548 U.S. 230, 248 (2006).

UAAAIWA v. Johnson Controls Inc.

Fighting for Women's Rights in the Workplace

ARGUED OCTOBER 10, 1990

STEVE LASH

Johnson Controls Inc. manufactures batteries whose assembly process entails exposure to high levels of lead. After discovering that eight of its female employees had become pregnant while maintaining blood lead levels in excess of those thought safe by the Occupational Safety and Health Administration (OSHA), Johnson barred all its female employees except those with medically documented infertility from engaging in tasks that require exposure to lead in excess of recommended OSHA levels. Following the implementation of Johnson's fetal-protection policy, the United Automobile Workers (UAW) challenged it as sexually discriminatory, in violation of Title VII of the 1964 Civil Rights Act. When the appellate court affirmed a district court decision in favor of Johnson, the UAW appealed, and the Supreme Court granted certiorari.

To listen to passages from oral arguments indicated with 🔊, visit www.goodquarrel.com.

RAREST AT THE SUPREME COURT IS THE ORAL ARGUMENT IN which the attorneys are at the top of their game, most of the justices are thoroughly engaged, and the case presents an issue in which both sides can—and do—argue convincingly that not only the law but also sound public policy is on their side.

Such was the case on the morning of October 10, 1990, when attorneys Marsha S. Berzon and Stanley S. Jaspan battled before the justices in *United Automobile, Aerospace, and Agricultural Implement Workers of America v. Johnson Controls Inc.* (1991),[1] which concerned whether a maker of car batteries could exclude women of childbearing age from working in areas that would expose them to lead, a central ingredient in batteries that is potentially harmful to fetuses. The policy was established when eight women in the plant became pregnant while maintaining blood lead levels that exceeded the safe level as established by OSHA. The policy barred all women, except for those who had documented proof of their inability to bear children, from any job that could result in exposure to lead.

Berzon, representing a group of the excluded women, argued that the federal law banning gender discrimination on the job required companies to allow women to work wherever men were permitted, even at potential risk to the unborn. That law, Title VII of the 1964 Civil Rights Act, left to women, not their employers, the informed choice about whether to work in areas that could harm fetuses, she said. Specifically, a group of women whose employment had been affected by the policy filed a class-action lawsuit in the U.S. District Court for the Eastern District of Wisconsin.

Berzon's argument adroitly not only focused on the text of the statute but addressed the law's goal of ending paternalistic company policies that ostensibly were designed to protect women but that in fact prevented them from climbing the corporate ladder. Berzon's skillful melding of statutory interpretation and public policy strengthened both elements of her argument.

---

1. 499 U.S. 187.

> The fetal-risk policies of this kind . . . if upheld, would keep women from a broad range of jobs because there are, in fact, a broad range of jobs that present potential fetal risks due to toxics but also due to disease, stress, noise, radiation and also to ordinary physical accidents, like car accidents, falls, etc. . . . The net effect of upholding a policy of this type, therefore, would be to sanction the resegregation of the workforce, particularly because the economics of the situation are that employers are going to instill fetal-protection policies in instances in which they are not dependent on women workers for their workforce and not instigate them where they are highly dependent on women workers, because then they would have nobody to do the job.

Jaspan, pressing the battery maker's case, countered that companies have an overriding legal and moral duty to protect workers and their potential offspring from known hazards, even if that means excluding a specific class of workers—in this case, women—from certain jobs. A company's need to prevent toxic exposure that could likely cause birth defects trumps the argument that the civil rights law requires an employer to place fertile women in harm's way, Jaspan said in an argument that also skillfully combined statutory interpretation and sound public policy. "We're not to leave common sense at the doorstep when interpreting Title VII," Jaspan argued. "It would violate common sense and the overriding interest in occupational health and safety to require an employer to damage unborn children."

Many of the nine justices were as engaged—and appeared as divided—as the attorneys during the hourlong argument. Justice Antonin G. Scalia illustrated one side of the debate. "One of the things that troubles me . . . about the case is that it seems to me unlikely that Congress is going to adopt a standard that whipsawed . . . the employer, that put him between a rock and a hard place," Scalia told Berzon. "That is to say, if he allows the women to take the jobs, he is subject to enormous suits for damages and maybe even punitive damages if the child is born deformed, and if he doesn't he's punished under Title VII."

But Scalia noted that in 1978, Congress amended Title VII with the Pregnancy Discrimination Act (PDA) specifically to address job discrimination against women based either on their pregnancy or their ability to become pregnant. "In interpreting the Pregnancy Discrimination Act, as you just have, that is, as making an exception, or considering it part of the job qualification that you not harm the fetus's health, it seems to me you're making a dead letter of it." Scalia told Jaspan. "That was always the justification used for discriminating against pregnant women, that they shouldn't work extralong hours because it would be bad for the fetus. I mean, to continue to allow that exception is to make a farce of the Pregnancy Discrimination Act. What other bases of treating pregnant women specially were there, except that it's bad for the child. You're making it a ridiculous piece of legislation."

Women of childbearing age could work near lead only if they submitted to the company a letter from a physician stating that they were sterile. Among the women who sued the company in the U.S. District Court for Eastern Wisconsin were Mary Craig, who said she opted for sterilization to avoid losing her job, and fifty-year-old divorcée Elsie Nason, who said she was transferred from a job that exposed her to lead to a lower-paying position.

The district court dismissed the lawsuit before trial, ruling that, as a matter of law, Johnson Controls was justified by "business necessity" in excluding women because of the threat lead exposure posed to fetuses. The court said that the women had failed to show the company could have adopted an alternative policy that would protect fetuses.[2]

The Seventh U.S. Circuit Court of Appeals upheld the dismissal. In its 7-4 vote, the Chicago-based court ruled that the fetal-protection policy was reasonably necessary for achieving the company's goal of industrial safety and that the women had not presented an adequate alternative. Due to the potential for severe harm to fetuses, "more is at stake" than a woman's general right not to be excluded from a job because of her ability to become pregnant, the court surmised.[3] Dissenting Seventh Circuit judges said that the case should not have been summarily dismissed, adding that the women should have had an opportunity

2. 886 F.2d 871, 886 (1989).

3. 886 F.2d 871, 897 (1989).

to prove at trial that the company's gender-based exclusion was barred under Title VII. The federal law prohibits companies from excluding women from jobs except in rare circumstances when being a man is a "bona fide occupational qualification reasonably necessary to the normal operation" of a business. That determination of necessity should be made only after a trial on the merits, the dissenters said.[4]

Appealing the Seventh Circuit's decision before the Supreme Court, Berzon argued that Johnson Controls's policy was not justified by business necessity as defined by the statute. She forcefully assailed the company, saying that its view of women harkened to a less-enlightened age when a male-dominated, pre–Title VII America presumed women incapable of making decisions for themselves, including the decision of when to become pregnant. "In today's day and age, women in general can control whether or not they are going to have children, and, therefore, in supposing that they will not, the policy is incorporating a negative behavioral stereotype," she said. She continued by noting that "the effect is that women will end up in the jobs where they began before Title VII was passed—that is, in child care centers, hospital nurses, teachers—not because there are fewer fetal risks in those jobs but because those are the jobs in which [women] are indispensable. The net effect is that this policy, if upheld, would cut the heart out of Title VII and out of the Pregnancy Discrimination Act."

Fetal-protection policies also present a "stigmatic harm" to women that the federal laws were designed to prevent, Berzon said, again mixing statutory interpretation and the public good. The policies subject women to "embarrassment and humiliation because of their private reproductive functions being made public," she added. "That is, everyone in the plant knows which women are fertile and which women are not fertile by which jobs they are placed in."

Having argued that the company's restrictions flout Title VII and public policy, Berzon then brought in the kicker argument that Johnson Controls's policy in fact undercuts its stated goal of protecting fetal health. By barring women from hazardous, better-paying jobs, Johnson

4. 886 F.2d 871, 902 (1989).

Controls was actually increasing the risk that the children of their female employees would be born with birth defects, Berzon said. Women in these dangerous but higher-paying positions have more money to save for when they do become pregnant. These additional funds can go toward paying for important prenatal treatment, which medical experts say helps prevent congenital abnormalities, Berzon argued. "If many employers adopt fetal-protection policies . . . the net result will be that many women will not have adequate income and will be relegating their children to precisely those fetal harms which Congress was in fact trying to prevent in passing the Pregnancy Discrimination Act," Berzon said. "Obviously, an employer is welcome and ought to be protecting fetal health to the highest degree possible, as long as he doesn't exclude women from the workplace."

But Justice Anthony M. Kennedy appeared unconvinced, stating that public policy and state law might in fact be on the employer's side. Just as strong as the need to prohibit discrimination based on pregnancy is the state's goal in ensuring that companies protect their workers to the fullest extent possible from known workplace hazards, he said. In response, Berzon argued that a company's obligation is to warn employees of the known risks of a job, including potential harm to fetuses. But Title VII prevents the employer from taking the additional step of barring women from that job, she said. Ultimately, for Berzon, the federal government, through the civil rights law, has shown that it trusts women to act in the best interest of their unborn children.

JUSTICE KENNEDY: Well, I don't think it's bizarre to assume that a state court in a tort suit would impose very severe liability on an employer for knowingly placing the woman in the position where the fetus is injured if the fetus is actually injured. If we can assume that for the moment, is it your position that any such liability should be preempted—

MS. BERZON: It's my position.

JUSTICE KENNEDY: By reason of a decision that's in your favor here?

MS. BERZON: That is precisely what a series of cases that this court has affirmatively cited held.

JUSTICE KENNEDY: But is it your position—

MS. BERZON: And it is my position, and it's also the employer's position, by the way.

JUSTICE KENNEDY: So your—your position is that a failure to find a BFOQ [bona fide occupational qualification] and a requirement that the employer be placed—that the employee have the position should preempt any tort liability for any injury to the fetus?

MS. BERZON: It's my position, and it is also the employer's position. Not any tort liability. Any tort liability for behavior which is not negligent or the warning—

JUSTICE KENNEDY: Not negligent, yes.

MS. BERZON: Yes—which is not negligent and where there were adequate warnings.

JUSTICE KENNEDY: So that in your position, the fetus should not be able to recover, or the newly born child, absent negligence?

MS. BERZON: That's correct.

JUSTICE SCALIA: You'd allow recovery against the mother who—who put the fetus in that position, I presume?

MS. BERZON: That assumes that the mother would be negligent if she put the fetus in that position, and, for the reasons that I stated earlier, that is an extremely unlikely context. And it's also true that the, again, the theory in which the mother could become liable does not yet exist, and I would argue strongly against it largely because—and as I was about to say—the woman herself is a decision maker in this situation, and the woman is—

JUSTICE KENNEDY: So there's—so there's no possible grounds for recovery for the injured child under your view?

MS. BERZON: I think that would be correct. On the other hand, as I was about to say, we are assuming a level of fetal injuries here that excludes the fact that women are going to act responsibly and that society in general, as this Court said emphatically in *Parham v. JR*, places in the hands of parents the responsibility to save their children from risk, recognizing that sometimes—occasionally they will make mistakes, but that if they do make mistakes or if a problem develops along that way, one does not put in the hands of a private individual the decision whether they ought to be overridden.

> It's the government that ordinarily has the power to override parental decisions, not the government. Nothing in this case implicates that relationship and would prevent OSHA or some other agency or the Congress from making determinations of that kind. The only issue here is whether the employer can do it; and what's noteworthy is that the employer's position here is really, as Judge Easterbrook said below, a not-on-our-watch position. In other words, "We don't want to be tied into this harm. What happens to this fetus and the rest of the world is just not our problem." And that's why the woman is a much more, both traditional but also completely informed decision maker. She also knows her own personal situation as to whether she is likely to have a child or not.

Countering Berzon, Jaspan too presented an argument based as much on public policy as the law. Companies, regardless of the demands of Title VII, owe a duty to their employees to provide a work environment where they can do their jobs "safely and efficiently," Jaspan said. "I think it is clear that employers, manufacturers, have now long been told that they are responsible for the consequences of their manufacturing substances," he added. "Manufacturers are liable, responsible if they injure their employees, they injure the children of their employees, their customers, their neighbors and the environment."

But Justice Sandra Day O'Connor appeared unpersuaded by the liability argument. The federal government, via Title VII and the Pregnancy Discrimination Act, might have taken the ultimate decision regarding a female employee's risk of harming her unborn out of the company's hands and placed it in the woman's, O'Connor said. "It seems to me that you are not coming to grips with the effect of the Pregnancy Discrimination Act," O'Connor told Jaspan. "The PDA—which says that female employees affected by pregnancy shall be treated the same for all employment-related purposes as other persons not affected but similar in their ability or inability to work."

Jaspan held fast to his public-policy argument. Having the "ability" to work means being capable of doing a job "safely and efficiently" without endangering others, including the unborn, he said. Companies have an obligation to ensure safety while promoting efficiency, he added. "No employer goes out and hires employees who may be able to produce the product in some rapid fashion but if it causes injury to fellow employees, to the employee who's doing the work, to neighbors, to other third parties, certainly that individual does not have the ability to perform the job," Jaspan said. "So the language of ability to perform the job, as expressed in the Pregnancy Discrimination Act, certainly includes the ability to perform it safely as well as efficiently."

Turning from an argument based on public policy to one rooted in the law, Jaspan said that Title VII permits discrimination against women if gender is a bona fide occupational qualification reasonably necessary to a business's normal operation. "The normal operation of manufacturers today is to provide for the health and safety of their employees, the children of their employees, and their neighbors and other third parties," Jaspan said. "To suggest that normal operation does not include concern for health and safety would certainly be a strange notion to most manufacturers today."

Jaspan added that the fetal-protection policy was based not on any discriminatory intent against women but on the sound workplace goal of health and safety. "The medical consultants unanimously said, 'Look, you're doing all of these other things; you're being irresponsible in exposing these [unborn] children to these levels of lead,'" Jaspan said. "An employer, a manufacturer, that creates a hazard has an obligation to protect against injury from that hazard. The employer here is simply exercising its obligations and its rights consistent with its normal operations as permitted by the bona fide occupational qualification defense."

Jaspan then directly took on Berzon's argument that Johnson Controls's policy should be relegated to the past, when women were viewed as incapable of making their own decisions.

> What clearly must be shown, and the reason why the abuse that seems to be suggested by petitioners that might occur from a decision affirming the court of appeals simply is not true, is that we're dealing with sound medical evidence. We're not dealing with stereotypes. We're not dealing with situations.

On March 20, 1991, the Supreme Court ruled that Johnson Controls's fetal-protection policy discriminated against women, in violation of Title VII of the 1964 Civil Rights Act as amended by the 1978 Pregnancy Discrimination Act. All nine justices found the policy illegal. A five-justice majority, led by Harry A. Blackmun, found fetal-protection policies unlawful in all cases. "Concern for a woman's existing or potential offspring historically has been the excuse for denying women equal employment opportunities," Blackmun wrote. "Congress in the PDA prohibited discrimination on the basis of a woman's ability to become pregnant. We do no more than hold that the Pregnancy Discrimination Act means what it says."[5] Joining Blackmun's opinion were O'Connor and Justices Thurgood Marshall, John Paul Stevens, and David H. Souter.

Three justices, led by White, held that a fetal-protection policy could be justified if the company can show the gender-based restriction is reasonably necessary to the normal operation of the business. For example, a company could justify a fetal-protection policy as a necessary protection against liability from a person born with a birth defect due to a mother's exposure to hazardous materials in the workplace. "[A]voidance of substantial safety risks to third parties is inherently part of both an employee's ability to perform a job and an employer's 'normal operation' of its business," White wrote. "[C]osts are relevant in determining whether a discriminatory policy is reasonably necessary for the normal operation of a business."[6] But Johnson Controls had failed to show that its restrictive policy against all fertile women was necessary to normal business operations insofar as the company had faced no liability before it adopted the policy in 1982. Joining White's opinion were Kennedy and Chief Justice William H. Rehnquist.

Scalia stated in a separate concurring opinion that a company's cost of reducing the risk of harm to a female employee's unborn could be so prohibitive as to justify a no-cost policy that simply excludes women on the theory that the gender-based restriction is reasonably necessary to

5. 499 U.S. 187, 211 (1991).

6. 499 U.S. 187, 214–217 (1991).

the business's normal operation. Johnson Controls, however, never tried to justify its policy by arguing that reducing the workplace risk posed by lead would be too expensive, Scalia wrote.

In the end, the justices, like the skilled attorneys who argued before them, grappled with the legal and public policy issues of women's rights and employer obligations, and rights prevailed.

Time Inc. v. Hill

A Future President Makes His Case

ARGUED APRIL 27, 1966

FRED GRAHAM

In 1952, three escaped convicts took James Hill, his wife, and their five children hostage in their Whitemarsh, Pennsylvania, home. After nineteen hours, the family was released unharmed. The convicts were later apprehended in a violent clash with police during which two of them were killed. In 1953, Joseph Hays published a novel based on the Hill family's ordeal. When the novel was subsequently made into a play, Life magazine printed an article about the play that mirrored many of its inaccuracies concerning the Hill family's experience. Alleging that the magazine had deliberately misrepresented his story, Hill sought damages against Life. On appeal from an adverse ruling, the Appellate Division of the New York Supreme Court remanded for a new trial, where a reduced adverse ruling was imposed on Life. Following an unsuccessful appeal in the New York Court of Appeals, the Supreme Court granted Life's owner, Time Inc., certiorari.

To listen to passages from oral arguments indicated with 🔊, visit www.goodquarrel.com.

WHEN RICHARD NIXON ROSE IN THE SUPREME COURT TO ARGUE for the appellee in the case of *Time Inc. v. Hill* (1967),[1] more was at stake than the outcome of a constitutional case of first impression. To be sure, the central constitutional point at issue was an important one. The year was 1966, just two years after the Supreme Court had, in its landmark ruling in *New York Times v. Sullivan* (1964),[2] recognized sweeping constitutional defenses for the news media in libel cases. The *Time* case would determine whether the Supreme Court would extend similar First Amendment protections to the media in a growing number of lawsuits for damages brought under state tort laws designed to protect individuals' right of privacy.

When most cases are argued in the Supreme Court, the legal question or questions at issue are the sole focus of events—and indeed, the core constitutional issue in this case was one of substantial importance. But the appearance of the ever-controversial Nixon presented a series of subplots that swirled beneath the surface of the proceedings that day.

Would Nixon, a political creature who had not argued in court in decades, measure up in the Supreme Court? Would sparks fly between the former vice president and Chief Justice Earl Warren, two archenemies during their days as California politicians? Would Nixon's resentment of the press, immortalized by his rant to reporters that he was leaving politics and they would not have "Nixon to kick around any more" (Newton 2006, 396), prompt him to go overboard in arguing for a citizen who claimed that a magazine had published a false story about his family to make a profit? And finally, why was Nixon arguing the case, anyway? A talented young lawyer in Nixon's firm, Leonard Garment, had won a judgment and preserved it at every stage below, so why would courtroom neophyte Nixon take over in the last crucial round? Would it be seen as part of a strategy to rehabilitate the former vice president's image for another run for the presidency in 1968, a possible politicization of the case that might muddy its legal focus?

His case was an important one, growing out of increasing public

1. 385 U.S. 374.

2. 376 U.S. 254.

concerns that the ever-more-powerful news media would trample on the privacy rights of individuals in a competitive frenzy to boost circulation or ratings. The case had its beginning in 1952, when three escaped convicts invaded the home of Philadelphia suburbanite James Hill and took Hill and his family hostage. After a harrowing nineteen hours of imprisonment, the family was released unharmed. The experience inspired the publication of a best-selling novel, *The Desperate Hours,* in which the Hill family's names were changed but the story closely followed the Hills' ordeal. Early in 1955 a play based on the book, also called *The Desperate Hours,* was set to open on Broadway. *Life* magazine, Time Inc.'s flagship publication, decided to run a major article about the event. The Hill family had long since left Philadelphia in search of anonymity elsewhere, and *Life*'s editors rented the house where the Hills' hostage ordeal had taken place. Magazine staff photographed a series of reenactments using the actors who would play the roles of the family members in the Broadway production. The *Life* article identified the Hill family and proclaimed that the reenacted scenes were photographed in "the actual house where the Hills were besieged." The article did not disclose that some of the reenacted scenes had been changed for dramatic effect.

James Hill sued Time Inc. under a New York statute providing a cause of action to a person whose name or picture is used by another without consent for purposes of trade or advertising. A jury awarded damages to Hill, and a series of appeals ensued, producing numerous delays and eventually Nixon's appearance in the U.S. Supreme Court on April 27, 1966.

In those days, the six newspaper reporters who regularly covered the Supreme Court were assigned seats squeezed into the narrow space between the attorneys' tables and the justices' bench. My seat as the correspondent for the *New York Times* was just a few feet from Nixon, and as he waited for the justices to enter the courtroom, he seemed nervous and uncomfortable. I asked him how he had prepared for the argument, and he said, "I locked myself up in my office for two weeks. No phone calls. No interruptions. It takes a tremendous amount of concentration."

This solitary style later became familiar when Nixon was president, but at the time I wondered that he did not mention practicing his argument with colleagues acting as justices, a technique that has now become routine and is known as a "murder board." Whatever the peculiarities of Nixon's preparation, his performance before the Court proved sound and workman-like, well within the bounds of effective oral advocacy. Supreme Court observers continue to debate the importance (or unimportance) of oral arguments to the outcome of most cases (Segal and Spaeth 2002; Johnson, Wahlbeck, and Spriggs 2006). In Nixon's case, the outcome was influenced to an unusual degree by factors beyond the quality of his presentation in court.

The opening argument was presented by Nixon's adversary, Harold R. Medina Jr., the son and namesake of a revered federal judge. Early on, Medina slipped into his argument the fact that he had represented media clients for a quarter century, implying, perhaps, that his views on media law might be more informed than those of the First Amendment rookie on the other side, as one exchange between Medina and Justice Byron R. White illustrates.

JUSTICE WHITE: Do you mean that *Life* or *Time* could not just decide that a very interesting thing in the life of an ordinary government worker or an ordinary industrial worker, and follow him around against his consent for a week, and write up every detail of his life?

MR. MEDINA: Well, let me give you the test that I have used for twenty-five years with *Time* and *Life*. I have said, number 1, you have no right to use anybody's name or picture. Number 2, you can do it if there is a reason for it. All I am trying to do is articulate this reason . . . what the reason is. Now, if you have a reason for it, I think you can do it. If you haven't got a reason, you can't do it. The reason for the *Hill* case is reporting on the play.

Medina argued that the New York privacy law was unconstitutional on its face because it was overbroad and allowed the media to be punished for reporting publicly known facts. As a fallback, he argued that the judgment in this case was invalid because the jury was permitted to base liability on a finding that the *Life* article was false, without regard to whether it was deliberately or recklessly so. Both points came out in his response to a question by Justice Abe Fortas.

JUSTICE FORTAS: So really the only issue that we have before us is whether the New York statute either on its face or as applied to the *Life* magazine article violates the First Amendment. Isn't that right?

MR. MEDINA: That is quite true, Your Honor, except that the sole test that was utilized with the jury, it was a dual test, one was the motive to increase circulation, which to my mind is just crazy. Because to the question "Does any publisher have a motive to increase circulation?" any jury is going to say yes to that. You might just as well say, "Is your motive sitting on the bench to earn money?" Obviously you are being paid for it, but your motive is to be a judge, and so the motive to increase circulation proves nothing.

The other thing is truth or falsity. What I am going to be working up to is that you cannot constitutionally use that as a test in a right of privacy action. But I will come back to Your Honor's question later in that context if you will let me go on with the story.

Underlying both defenses was the argument that if this judgment was not unconstitutional, then persons who feel they have been defamed can perform an end run around the defenses established in *New York Times v. Sullivan* by suing for a violation of privacy. Medina pointed out the possibilities for a suit against the media for an innocent mistake: "It comes down to if you treat it on a mistake basis, on truth or falsity, what has happened to the law of libel? You don't need the law of libel any more and the safeguards. It is much easier to sue for violation of your right of privacy. But all the defenses that have been set up in the libel law disappear."

When Nixon rose to respond, it was immediately apparent that his manner would be properly professional, with none of the self-important posturing that the justices had witnessed when some other political figures had argued before them. He told the Court that in a string of cases extending for more than sixty years, the New York courts had construed the privacy law so narrowly that it imposed liability only when the defendant had fictionalized a story for trade or profit.

MR. NIXON: If it is a true account of a newsworthy event, then even though it goes back many, many years—referring earlier to Mr. Justice Fortas's question—then a true account incurs no liability. But it is only when the publisher falsifies, fictionalizes—the term used in the New York cases—the relationship between a past event and the plaintiff and falsifies for the purposes of trade in order, of course, to make it a more newsy, salable article, it is then only that liability incurs.

JUSTICE FORTAS: You don't get that from a statute; you get that from the cases, I assume?

MR. NIXON: Mr. Justice Fortas, the statute states basically a liability on the basis of two tests: One, advertising, which is relatively clear, the use of an ad. Even there, there are exceptions. But second, for the purposes of trade. Now, if "for purposes of trade" had not been, over a period of sixty years, very narrowly interpreted by the New York statutes to include only those instances where there had been falsification amounting to fictionalization, this statute, I believe, would be subject to constitutional question.

JUSTICE FORTAS: What case are you relying on?

MR. NIXON: The New York cases, going back over a period of years, have held that where there is a true account, a true account of a past situation, that there is no liability. The leading case in that respect is the *Sidis* case, a case which involved actually a very sad situation. A genius who was newsworthy at the time was giving instructions when he was eleven years old to people in higher mathematics at Harvard, and then, with the sensitivity sometimes characteristic of genius, retreating into private life; a quarter of a century later, [his tale was] dug up by the *New Yorker* magazine, and a story written about him, the story entitled "April Fool"—he had been born on April Fool's Day. Yet the New York court, as an indication of its concern for the First Amendment, in this case refused to hold the publication liable on the ground that it was a true account of what had been a newsworthy event and in which there was still an interest in news.

By definition, he said, a fictionalized story is not news, and thus freedom of the press is not affected by the law. Justice White saw a problem with that argument.

JUSTICE WHITE: As the New York statute comes to us, however, it would cover the situation where the story about the past event was false, but it was only negligently false, for example—or we might say it was an excusable error, but it was nevertheless false—you would say New York would impose liability in that case?

MR. NIXON: Mr. Justice White, I believe New York would impose liability in such a case. I know of no New York case where that has happened.

Slightly rattled, the former vice president hastened to add a line that Nixon the politician had often employed in the rough-and-tumble of political debate: "But let me make one thing very clear." At that point, White cut Nixon off.

In fact, Nixon the Supreme Court advocate was at times candid to a fault. Under questioning by the justices, he conceded points that a cannier counsel might have deflected with obfuscation or guile. It was as if Nixon feared that if he came across as too cunning, he might underscore his "Tricky Dick" reputation from his political days, and he responded with candor that at times seemed to concede more than necessary.

Nixon's basic argument was that the privacy law did not pose a threat to free expression because it required "fictionalization" to be actionable. Doesn't this mean, Justice Abe Fortas asked, that a newspaper could publish accurate photos of the intimacies of a married couple without violating the privacy law? Nixon conceded, "That would be my conclusion." Justice Fortas asked, "Did I understand you a little earlier to volunteer the statement *Life* had carefully checked this story, or that they had a practice of carefully checking?" Nixon conceded, "Yes."

Fortas followed up: "That may leave you with the problem in the event we don't agree" with your argument that fictionalization is the heart of the case. Nixon replied, "That is correct." Chief Justice Warren confronted Nixon with the ultimate issue in the case: if the Court were to reject the argument that proof of fictionalization decides the case, wouldn't that mean that the privacy law raises a potential threat to the First Amendment? Nixon responded, "I would say it would. I am referring now not to the New York cases. I am referring to the whole field of privacy, which will be before this Court I am sure in times in the future. . . . I believe that if the lines are drawn too tightly, that you would have a serious restriction of freedom of expression."

Warren gave no hint from the bench of his ancient enmity toward Nixon, and Warren's remarks in fact suggested that he was sympathetic toward Nixon's side of the case. But Warren drew titters from the courtroom by catching Nixon off base on a point of California law. Nixon had tried to explain away a California court decision by declaring that "in California this was a common-law decision, there was no statute in California."

CHIEF JUSTICE WARREN: Do we have common-law jurisdiction out there?

MR. NIXON: I think it is common-law jurisdiction. That is my recollection—pardon me, I am sorry. Under the California Code—

Warren settled back in his chair with a satisfied smile.

There were also signals from the bench that day that another of the Court's liberals, Fortas, was also sympathetic to Nixon's side of the case. At times Fortas seemed to play devil's advocate, but mostly his questions seemed calculated to help Nixon frame the strongest possible case that the media can constitutionally be held liable for abuse of individuals' privacy.

In fact, Supreme Court papers made public in recent years have disclosed that when the justices met in their conference after the argument, Fortas was in a majority that voted to uphold Nixon's side of the case. Warren, who was also in the majority, assigned the opinion to Fortas, who drafted a majority opinion that bitterly denounced the "needless, heedless, wanton and deliberate injury" inflicted by *Life* magazine in this case. But by then it was early June. Fortas's majority was not firm, and the Court was rushing toward adjournment. The case was put over for reargument early in the next term.

When the case came up for reargument in October, the novelty of Nixon's participation had worn off. He was much more confident and knowledgeable in the second argument, but there was a sense that the justices had to strain to keep the dialogue in motion. In those days, each side was permitted to argue for an hour (the justices have since prudently reduced that to a half hour), and because the reargument began late in the day, the Court recessed in midargument and all parties returned the next morning to finish the job.

In fact, it became apparent early in the reargument that a majority of the justices were inclined to require some form of the *New York Times v. Sullivan* defenses in privacy cases. Medina urged the Court to strike the law down on its face because "[i]n this field of privacy, I merely suggest that when it is nondefamatory and when you are talking about a public fact, we should have the protection that the fellow who comes in to sue us must prove both falsity and knowledge of falsity, or recklessness, and that this is a minimum, because, mind you, this article here, the dissent in the appellate division, found it was an informative presentation of legitimate news."

Nixon responded, "It is our contention that in this case it was argued by the plaintiff, it was established by the evidence, it was charged by the court, it was found by the jury, and it was held by the courts of New York in their appeals courts, that *Life* magazine lied, and that *Life* magazine knew that it lied. That is the proposition that I contend for here." But Nixon was on the defensive because the trial judge had not instructed the jury that it must find knowledge of falsity or recklessness to render a judgment against *Life.*

The reargument ended with Medina insisting that even if the record indicated that *Life*'s editors knew of the falsity of their article, because the jury had not been instructed on the necessity of finding intentional, knowing falsity, "I still think I am entitled to win."

After the reargument but before the Court issued its decision, Nixon's cause suffered a stunning setback. New York's highest court issued a decision that implied that under the state's privacy statute, liability could be upheld without proof of knowing or reckless falsity, a view of the law that the Supreme Court would almost certainly declare unconstitutional. Even though Nixon had not had an opportunity to respond to the new decision in oral argument, this eleventh-hour development became a major element in the Supreme Court's subsequent opinion, in which the Court reversed the judgment against *Life* magazine.

In an opinion written by Justice William J. Brennan Jr., the Court held that privacy suits are subject to the same constitutional defenses as libel actions. The Court declined to strike down the New York privacy law on its face but overturned the jury's award because the judge had not had the prescience to include the new defenses in his charge. Nixon's cause lost by a margin of 5-4, with Fortas writing the dissent.

Two years later, on the last day Warren appeared on the Court before his retirement, Nixon rose to deliver an unprecedented address to the Court by a sitting president. Nixon began a warm tribute to Warren's tenure as chief justice by joking that based on Nixon's two arguments before the Court in the *Hill* case, the only ordeal more challenging than a presidential press conference was an argument before the Supreme Court.

ACKNOWLEDGMENTS

This book could not have been written without the help of many people. Authors often thank their editors last. Here we do just the opposite. We give our warmest thanks to Jim Reische at the University of Michigan Press, because without his enthusiasm for our project, Michigan would not have taken it on, and without his unrelenting desire to see this project through, we would not have completed it. Since Jim left the Press, we are indebted to Melody Herr, Scott Griffith, and Kevin Rennells for guiding us through the publication process. We also thank the reporters who contributed to this volume. They deserve enormous credit for signing on to an initially amorphous concept. The work they put in to make the essays interesting and readable is commendable. Without the efforts of these eleven, this volume would not have reached fruition.

Tim thanks Jerry Goldman for his mentoring, patience, and unwavering belief in Tim as a coauthor, colleague, and co–principal investigator on our National Science Foundation project. Tim also thanks Ryan Black, Jim Spriggs, and Paul Wahlbeck for always listening to his ideas and for the excellent feedback on his thoughts as this book was in the making. In addition, Paul Goren, Joanne Miller, Jason Roberts, Sarah Treul, and Justin Wedeking provided assistance and advice throughout this book's gestation. Tim also thanks Abby Bar-Lev, Chris Galdieri, Serena Laws, and Jessica Schroeder for their excellent research assistance at the University of Minnesota. Finally, he again thanks Julie, Alexi, Aidan, and Satchel for their patience as he has worked on this project.

Jerry is enormously grateful to many people. In a profession that assiduously resists change, a few brave colleagues offered key support along the way. Lee Epstein (now at Northwestern Law School) and Tom Walker (at Emory University) were early enthusiasts. Beyond the academic world, Tim Stanley and Stacy Stern (both of Justia) have been generous with their time and ideas in support of free public access to legal materials. They provided needed encouragement a decade ago, when this volume was conceived. Jeff Parsons, lead technology consultant and friend, has been a prolific source of excellent technical and substantive ideas and has shared the skills needed to put those ideas into practice. Chris Karr kept the project afloat as he pushed and prodded the archive of cases at Oyez.org to a unified content management system. Jerry's legions of students made enormous contributions to this project, but a few stand out for special acknowledgment: Andrew Gruen, Andrew Hernacki, Susan MacDougall, Jason Wagner, and Jessica Wash. Jerry also expresses his gratitude to Susan Kennedy and their two dogs, Jack and Luna, for their tolerance and good cheer during the long birthing process of *A Good Quarrel.*

Finally, both of us thank the National Science Foundation for its support of our collaborative work gathering, digitizing, and disseminating Supreme Court arguments on the World Wide Web. The support came through grants IIS-0324992 and IIS-0325282.

WORKS CITED

ABC News. 2000. *Nightline*. December 13.

Abramowitz, Alan I. 1995. "It's Abortion, Stupid: Policy Voting in the 1992 Presidential Election." *Journal of Politics* 57 (1): 176–86.

Biskupic, Joan. 2005. *Sandra Day O'Connor: How the First Woman on the Supreme Court Became Its Most Influential Justice*. New York: HarperCollins.

Brandeis, Louis. 1933. *Other People's Money and How the Bankers Use It*. Whitefish, Mont.: Kessinger.

Champoux, Mark. 2006. "Uncovering Coherence in Compelled Subsidy of Speech Doctrine." *Harvard Journal of Law and Public Policy* 29 (summer): 1107–17.

Clement, Paul. 2006. Brief for the United States, Rapanos v. U.S., January 13.

Denniston, Lyle. 1990. "Souter Confirmation Expected Despite Lingering Feminist Opposition." *Baltimore Sun,* September 25.

Denniston, Lyle. 1991. "Pa. Abortion Case Sets Stage for Test of Roe vs. Wade; High Court Review Possible by Summer." *Baltimore Sun,* November 8.

Denniston, Lyle. 1992. "Administration Brief Asks High Court to Overturn Roe vs. Wade Completely." *Baltimore Sun,* April 7.

Enns, Krista M. 1998. "Note: Can a California Litigant Prevail in an Action for Legal Malpractice Based on an Attorney's Oral Argument before the U.S. Supreme Court?" *Duke Law Journal* 48 (October): 111–46.

Galloway, Russell. 1989. "Oral Argument in the Court." *Trial* 25 (1): 78–84.

Greenhouse, Linda. 1992. "Abortion Rights Strategy: All or Nothing." *New York Times,* April 23.

Greenhouse, Linda. 2005. *Becoming Justice Blackmun: Harry Blackmun's Supreme Court Journey.* New York: Times Books/Henry Holt.

Harlan, John. 1955. "What Part Does the Oral Argument Play in the Conduct of an Appeal?" *Cornell Law Quarterly* 41 (1): 6–11.

Hughes, Charles Evans. 1928. *The Supreme Court of the United States: Its Foundations, Methods, and Achievements: An Interpretation.* New York: Columbia University Press.

Johnson, Timothy R. 2004. *Oral Arguments and Decision Making on the United States Supreme Court.* Albany: SUNY Press.

Johnson, Timothy R., James F. Spriggs, and Paul J. Wahlbeck. 2007. "Oral Advocacy before the United States Supreme Court: Does It Affect Justices' Decisions?" *Washington University Law Review* 85 (3): 457–527.

Johnson, Timothy R., Paul J. Wahlbeck, and James F. Spriggs. 2006. "The Influence of Oral Arguments on the U.S. Supreme Court." *American Political Science Review* 100 (1): 99–113.

Kolbert, Kathryn, et al. 1992. Planned Parenthood of Southeastern Pennsylvania v. Casey, Brief for Petitioners and Cross Respondents.

Mauro, Tony. 1997. "Fruit Fight." *Legal Times,* September 29.

Mauro, Tony. 1998. "Bitter Fruit." *Legal Times,* February 10.

Mauro, Tony. 2006. "Congress Focuses on Cameras at the High Court." *Legal Times,* April 3.

McConnell, Michael. 1996. Letter to Supreme Court clerk William K. Suter. December 4.

Moody, James A. 1998. Affidavit. *The Law Firm of Thomas E. Campagne and Associates v. Gerawan Farming, Inc.* May 5.

Newton, Jim. 2006. *Justice for All: Earl Warren and the Nation He Made.* New York: Riverhead.

O'Brien, David M. 2000. *Storm Center.* New York: Norton.

O'Connor, Sandra Day. 1989. *Webster v. Reproductive Health Services* 492 U.S. 522.

Rehnquist, William. 2001. *The Supreme Court: How It Was, How It Is.* 2nd ed. New York: Morrow.

Rehnquist, William. 1984. "Oral Advocacy: A Disappearing Art." *Mercer Law Review* 34 (summer): 1015–28.

Rehnquist, William. 1986. "Oral Advocacy." *South Texas Law Review* 27 (summer): 289–303.

Remsen, Nancy. 2006. "Lawyers Prepare to Face High Court." *Burlington Free Press,* February 9.

Savage, David. 1992. "The Rescue of Roe vs. Wade: How a Dramatic Change of Heart by a Supreme Court Justice Affirmed the Right to Abortion—Just When the Issue Seemed Headed for Certain Defeat." *Los Angeles Times,* December 13.

"Scalia Attacks Church-State Court Rulings." 2003. *New York Times,* January 13.

Scalia, Antonin. 2005. Interview. *Constitutional Conversation.* Washington, D.C.: C-SPAN.

Segal, Jeffrey A., and Harold J. Spaeth. 2002. *The Supreme Court and the Attitudinal Model Revisited.* New York: Cambridge University Press.

Stern, Robert L., Eugene Gressman, and Stephen M. Shapiro. 1993. *Supreme Court Practice: For Practice in the Supreme Court of the United States.* 7th ed. Washington, D.C.: Bureau of National Affairs.

Wasby, Stephen L., Anthony A. D'Amato, and Rosemary Metrailer. 1976. "The Functions of Oral Argument in the U.S. Supreme Court." *Quarterly Journal of Speech* 62 (4): 410–22.

White, Byron. 1982. "The Work of the Supreme Court." *New York State Bar Journal* 54 (October): 346–83.

CONTRIBUTORS

CHARLES BIERBAUER has been dean of the College of Mass Communications and Information Studies at the University of South Carolina since 2002. He served as CNN's senior Washington correspondent and reported on the U.S. Supreme Court from 1997 to 2001.

LYLE DENNISTON is a Supreme Court correspondent who regularly contributes to scotusblog.com and Radio WBUR in Boston.

JERRY GOLDMAN heads the OYEZ Project, a multimedia relational database devoted to the U.S. Supreme Court (http://www.oyez.org). He is also a recipient of the 1997 EDUCOM Medal and the 1998 Silver Gavel Award of the American Bar Association for improving public understanding of law. In 2005, the department of political science at Northwestern University awarded him the Farrell Teaching Prize for his long commitment to undergraduate teaching and advising.

FRED GRAHAM is a legal journalist who has reported on the Supreme Court for more than forty years, beginning with the *New York Times* in 1965. He shifted to CBS News in 1972 and moved to Court TV in 1990. He now serves as senior editor of Court TV, based in Washington, D.C.

TIMOTHY R. JOHNSON holds a doctorate from Washington University in St. Louis. He is the author of *Oral Arguments and Decision Making on the U.S.*

Supreme Court (2004) and the coauthor, with Chris Gilbert, David A. M. Peterson, and Paul Djupe, of *Religious Institutions and Minor Parties in the United States* (1999).

BRENT KENDALL has covered the Supreme Court for the *Los Angeles Daily Journal* and the *San Francisco Daily Journal* since 2003.

STEVE LASH has reported on the Supreme Court since 1989 for several publications, including the *Chicago Daily Law Bulletin, Houston Chronicle,* Cox Newspapers, and *West's Legal News.* He is a member of the Supreme Court and Maryland bars.

RICHARD LAZARUS is a professor of law at Georgetown University and serves as faculty director of the Supreme Court Institute, which helps counsel prepare for oral argument before the Supreme Court. He has represented the United States, state and local governments, and environmental groups before the U.S. Supreme Court in thirty-nine cases and has presented oral argument in twelve of those cases.

DAHLIA LITHWICK is a senior editor and legal correspondent for Slate.com, where she writes and edits the columns "Supreme Court Dispatches" and "Jurisprudence." She has covered the Microsoft trial, *Bush v. Gore,* the Roberts and Alito confirmations, and other legal issues.

TONY MAURO has covered the Supreme Court since 1979, first for Gannett News Service and *USA Today* and since January 2000 for American Lawyer Media. In that capacity he covers the Court for *Legal Times, American Lawyer Magazine,* and other publications and for law.com.

TIM O'BRIEN covered the U.S. Supreme Court for ABC News from 1977 to 2000. He currently serves as a distinguished visiting professor at Nova–Southeastern University School of Law in Fort Lauderdale, Florida.

DAVID G. SAVAGE has covered the Supreme Court and legal issues for the *Los Angeles Times* since 1986. He is the author of *Turning Right: The Making of the Rehnquist Supreme Court* (1992).

GREG STOHR has covered legal issues for Bloomberg News in Washington, D.C., since 1996, focusing primarily on the U.S. Supreme Court since 1998. He won the 2001 New York Press Club Spot News Award for his coverage of *Bush v. Gore*. His book, *A Black and White Case: How Affirmative Action Survived Its Greatest Legal Challenge* (2004) examines the University of Michigan admissions cases resolved by the Supreme Court in 2003.

NINA TOTENBERG serves as National Public Radio's legal affairs correspondent, contributing reports to the critically acclaimed newsmagazines *All Things Considered, Morning Edition,* and *Weekend Edition*. Her work has won numerous awards.

INDEX

Abood v. Detroit Board of Education, 79, 79n4
abortion, 8, 34; informed consent for, 42, 45. See also *Planned Parenthood of Southeastern Pennsylvania v. Casey;* women
ACLU. *See* American Civil Liberties Union
Act 64, 145
Adams, John Quincy, vii
advertising. See *Glickman v. Wileman Brothers and Elliott Inc.*
advocacy. *See* oral advocacy
affirmative action, 26, 36, 107. See also *Grutter v. Bollinger; Regents of the University of California v. Alan Bakke*
African Americans, 22, 25, 104, 106
Agricultural Marketing Agreement Act (AMAA), 74, 81
agriculture. *See* Agricultural Marketing Agreement Act
Alito, Samuel A., Jr. (associate justice), 10, 131; as judge on the circuit court, 45–46; on *Rapanos v. United States,* 132
Al Odah v. United States, 3
AMAA. *See* Agricultural Marketing Agreement Act
America and the Courts, 41
American Civil Liberties Union (ACLU), 43
Antifederalists, 126
"April Fool," 174–75
Arberg, Kathy, 62
Army Corps of Engineers. *See* U.S. Army Corps of Engineers
Ashcroft, John (senator), 130
atheism, 18

ballots. See *Bush v. Gore*
Barrett, Richard, 8, 24, 31–36; misconduct, 25–26
Berzon, Marsha S., 159–68
Bill of Rights, 43
Blackmun, Harry A. (justice): opinion on *Forsyth County, Georgia v. the Nationalist Movement,* 37–38; on *Roe v. Wade,* 46; on Title VII, 167
Boies, David, 62–66
Bopp, James, Jr., 148–50
Boumediene v. Bush, 3
Brandeis, Louis D. (justice), 41, 155
Brennan, William J. (justice): on abortion, 46–47; on oral arguments, 5
Breyer, Stephen G. (justice): on *Chandler v. Miller,* 123; in defense of the Pledge of Allegiance, 17–18; as dissenter in

Breyer, Stephen G. (*continued*)
Bush v. Gore, 67–68; on *Glickman v. Wileman Brothers and Elliott Inc.,* 86–87; on *Randall v. Sorrell,* 152–53, 157; on religion in the public school system, 17
Brown v. Board of Education, viii
Brunelle, Donald, 154
Buckley v. Valeo, 145, 146
Burger, Warren E. (chief justice), on oral arguments, 6, 6n3
Bush, George H. W. (president), 57, 60, 129
Bush, George W. (president), 61, 104, 130
Bush v. Gore, 3, 8–9, 26, 39, 40, 61–73; vote of the justices, 67–68
Bush v. Palm Beach County Canvassing Board, 61, 69–70

Cal-Almond, Inc. v. U.S. Department of Agriculture, 79–80, 79n5
California. See *Elk Grove Unified School District v. Newdow; Glickman v. Wileman Brothers and Elliott Inc.; Regents of the University of California v. Alan Bakke*
cameras, in the courtroom, 70–71
Campagne, Thomas, 75–76, 84–92
Carabell, June, 130
Carabell, Keith, 130
Carabell v. Army Corps, 130
Central Hudson Gas and Electric Corp. v. Public Service Commission, 78–79, 84
Chandler, Walker, 110, 111. See also *Chandler v. Miller*
Chandler v. Miller, 9, 110–24
Cheney, Richard B. (vice president), 61
church and state. See *Elk Grove Unified School District v. Newdow*
civil rights, demonstrations, 22–23
Civil Rights Act, 158, 159, 167
Clean Air Act, 129–30
Clean Water Act (CWA), 125, 127, 129–30, 131, 142
Clement, Paul D., 130–31, 139–40, 141–43
Clinton, Bill (president), 60, 77
courtroom: audio in, 71; cameras in, 70–71; reporters in, 71
Cox v. New Hampshire, 27, 32, 37
Craig, Mary, 161
C-SPAN, 1, 40, 41
CWA. *See* Clean Water Act

Days, Drew, III, 76–77
Dean, Howard (governor of Vermont), 146
Democrat Party v. Wisconsin, 120
demonstrations, 20. See also *Forsyth County, Georgia v. the Nationalist Movement*
The Desperate Hours, 171
DeVore, P. Cameron, 78, 94
diversity, value in higher education, 109. See also *Grutter v. Bollinger*
"Do or Die Day," 47
Douglas, William O. (justice), viii; on oral arguments, 6
Dred Scott decision, 25
drug testing. See *Chandler v. Miller*
Duke Law Journal, 93

Easterbrook, Judge, 165
"Edgar Ray Killen Appreciation Day," 38
education, 8. See also *Brown v. Board of Education; Elk Grove Unified School District v. Newdow*
elected officials, in public, 1
elections, 120; campaign finance, 145–57. *See also* presidential elections; *Randall v. Sorrell*
Eleventh U.S. Circuit Court of Appeals, 27
Elk Grove Unified School District v. Newdow, 8, 11–19
Enns, Krista, 93–94
environment, activists, 131. See also *Rapanos v. United States*
Environmental Protection Agency. *See* U.S. Environmental Protection Agency
Ewing, Thomas (general), viii
Ewing, Thomas (senator), viii

federal government, 9–10; federal power and water rights, 126–28; legal limitations of, 130–31; rights on waterways, 129. See also *Rapanos v. United States*
Fifth Amendment, 50

First Amendment, 11, 75; Establishment Clause, 11, 16; protection of, 77; violation of, 37. See also *Chandler v. Miller; Elk Grove Unified School District v. Newdow; Forsyth County, Georgia v. the Nationalist Movement; Glickman v. Wileman Brothers and Elliott Inc.; Randall v. Sorrell; Time Inc. v. Hill*
Flood v. Kuhn, 111n2
Florida Supreme Court. See *Bush v. Gore*
Forsyth County, Georgia v. the Nationalist Movement, 8, 20–41; opinions, 36–41; video of, 24–25
Forsyth County Board of Commissioners, 22–23
Fortas, Abe (justice), 10; on *Time Inc. v. Hill*, 173, 174, 175–76
Fourteenth Amendment, 50, 51
Fourth Amendment, 111, 117
Fresno Bee, 92

Garment, Leonard, 170
gender discrimination, 159. See also *United Automobile, Aerospace, and Agricultural Implement Workers of America (UAAAIWA) v. Johnson Controls Inc.*
George W. Bush and Richard Cheney v. Albert Gore et al., 71
Georgia. See *Chandler v. Miller; Forsyth County, Georgia v. the Nationalist Movement*
Gerawan, Dan, 77, 92, 93–94
Gerawan Farming, 77
Ginsburg, Ruth Bader (justice), 9; on *Chandler v. Miller*, 117; on children in the Supreme Court, 16; on *Glickman v. Wileman Brothers and Elliott Inc.*, 80–81; on *Grutter v. Bollinger*, 100–101, 103; on *Randall v. Sorrell*, 149; on *Rapanos v. United States*, 132, 136
Glickman, Dan, 76–77
Glickman v. Wileman Brothers and Elliott Inc., 9, 74–97
Goldberg, Arthur J. (justice), 111
Gore, Al (vice president), 61, 126
government, federal power and water rights, 126–28
Gratz, Jennifer, 109
Gratz v. Bollinger, 100
Greenhouse, Linda, 44
Grutter, Barbara, 98, 100
Grutter v. Bollinger, 9, 98–109
Guilday, Patricia, 9, 120–24

Hamdi v. Rumsfeld, 3
Harlan, John Marshall, II (justice), on oral arguments, 5, 6–7
Harris, Katherine, 70
Harvard Journal of Law and Public Policy, 96
Harvard University, 107
Hays, Joseph, 169
Hill, James, 169, 171. See also *Time Inc. v. Hill*
Hispanic Americans, 104, 106
Hopper, M. Reed, 129–37
House, Toni, 2
House Appropriations Committee, 40

indigence, 29
Internet, 1, 4

Jackson, Robert H. (justice), on oral arguments, 4–5
Jaspan, Stanley S., 159–68
Jehovah's Witness, 27
Jenkins, Alan, 79–84
Johnson Controls Inc., 158, 161. See also *United Automobile, Aerospace, and Agricultural Implement Workers of America (UAAAIWA) v. Johnson Controls Inc.*
justices: calling by wrong names, 9; on oral arguments, viii, 4–7. *See also* individual Supreme Court justices

Keller v. State Bar of California, 80–81, 80n7
Kennedy, Anthony M. (justice), 8; on abortion, 51; on Article II in *Bush v. Gore*, 63–66; on *Chandler v. Miller*, 113–15, 117, 119; on children in the Supreme Court, 14–15; on diversity, 104; on *Glickman v. Wileman Brothers and Elliott Inc.*, 89; on *Grutter v. Bollinger*, 100–101, 102; on indigence,

Kennedy, Anthony M. (*continued*) 28; opinion on *Rapanos v. United States,* 143–44; on parade statute and fees, 33–34; on *Randall v. Sorrell,* 149–50; on *Rapanos v. United States,* 128, 135, 137, 141–42; on religion in the public school system, 16; on spousal-notice provision for abortion, 55–56; on Title VII, 163–64
Klock, Joseph, 70
Kolbert, Kathryn, 42–60
Kolbo, Kirk, 100, 101–3
Ku Klux Klan, 22

Legal Times, 4
Libertarian Party, 111. See also *Chandler v. Miller*
Life, 169, 171
Lincoln, Abraham, vii
Los Angeles Times, 4

Mahoney, Maureen, 99, 100, 105–9
"March against Fear and Intimidation," 22
Marshall, John (chief justice), vii
Marshall, Thurgood (justice), vii–viii; on abortion, 46–47; retirement, 25
Martin Luther King Jr. Day, 20, 22
Mayer, Brown, and Platt, 77
McConnell, Michael, 77, 92
media, 170. See also *Time Inc. v. Hill*
Medina, Harold R., Jr., 172–78
Michelman, Kate, 44, 60
Michigan. See *Grutter v. Bollinger; Rapanos v. United States*
Michigan Department of Environmental Quality, 125
migratory bird rule, 128, 135
Miller, Zell D., 110. See also *Chandler v. Miller*
Mintz, Morton, 39
misconduct, 26–27
Mississippi Burning, 3
Moody, James, 85, 94
Murdock v. Pennsylvania, 27–28, 32

Nason, Elsie, 161
National Abortion Rights Action League, 44
National Archives, 2
National Guard, 22
National Industrial Recovery Act, 82
Nationalist Movement, 8, 23; assets of, 28, 39. See also *Forsyth County, Georgia v. the Nationalist Movement*
National Organization for Women, 47
National Public Radio, 4
National Voting Rights Institute, 155
Native Americans, 106
New York, 147. See also *Time Inc. v. Hill*
New York Supreme Court, 169
New York Times, 171
New York Times v. Sullivan, 170, 173, 177
Ninth Circuit Court of Appeals, 13, 16
Nixon, Richard (president), vii, 10, 170. See also *Time Inc. v. Hill*

Occupational Safety and Health Administration (OSHA), 158, 165
O'Connor, Sandra Day (justice), 8, 9; on abortion, 48, 49, 52; on *Chandler v. Miller,* 112, 116–17, 118, 120–21; on diversity, 104–5; on *Glickman v. Wileman Brothers and Elliott Inc.,* 79–80, 88, 89–90; on *Grutter v. Bollinger,* 100; opinion on *Forsyth County, Georgia v. the Nationalist Movement,* 37; on oral arguments, 93; on parade statute and fees, 27–29; on the Pregnancy Discrimination Act, 165; on *Rapanos v. United States,* 128; on *Roe v. Wade,* 46; on spousal-notice provision for abortion, 54; on Title VII, 165
Olson, Ted, 62–63, 68, 104, 130
oral advocacy. *See* oral arguments
oral arguments, vii–ix, 4–7, 6n3; definitions, 111; good versus bad, 111; justices and, viii; Supreme Court and, viii–ix; "Ten Commandments of Oral Advocacy" in the Supreme Court, 8, 11–19. *See also* individual Supreme Court justices
Ordinance 34, 20, 22–23, 30–31. See also *Forsyth County, Georgia v. the Nationalist Movement*
OSHA. *See* Occupational Safety and Health Administration

Pacific Legal Foundation (PLF), 127–28, 128–29
"Page 13," 62
parade statute, 27, 28. See also *Forsyth County, Georgia v. the Nationalist Movement*
Parham v. JR, 164
Payton, John, 99
PDA. *See* Pregnancy Discrimination Act
Pennsylvania. See *Planned Parenthood of Southeastern Pennsylvania v. Casey; Time Inc. v. Hill*
Pennsylvania Abortion Control Act, 47
PG & E v. PUC of California, 90
Planned Parenthood Federation of America, 44
Planned Parenthood of Southeastern Pennsylvania v. Casey, 2, 8, 42–60
Pledge of Allegiance, 8, 11; defense of, 17–18. See also *Elk Grove Unified School District v. Newdow*
PLF. *See* Pacific Legal Foundation
police protection, 30–31
politics: 1992 election, 48; 2000 election, 62; U.S. Supreme Court and, 44–45
pollutants, 127, 138, 141–42; definition, 127
Powell, Lewis F., Jr. (justice): on affirmative action, 36; opinion in *Regents of the University of California v. Alan Bakke,* 98; on oral arguments, 5, 6
Preate, Ernest D., Jr., 53
pregnancy, 10. See also *United Automobile, Aerospace, and Agricultural Implement Workers of America (UAAAIWA) v. Johnson Controls Inc.;* women
Pregnancy Discrimination Act (PDA), 160–61, 163, 165, 167
presidential elections: 1992, 48; 2000, 62. See also *Bush v. Gore*
privacy, 10; U.S. Constitution and, 34. See also *Time Inc. v. Hill*
public permits, 20; fees, 20. See also *Forsyth County, Georgia v. the Nationalist Movement*
publishing, 10. See also *Time Inc. v. Hill*
Putin, Vladimir, 18

racism, 22, 98. See also *Grutter v. Bollinger*
Ralph Baze and Thomas C. Bowling, Petitioners v. John D. Rees, Commissioner, Kentucky Department of Corrections, et al., 3
Randall, Neil, 145
Randall v. Sorrell, 10, 145–57; decision, 156–57
Rankin, Jeannette, 43
Rapanos, John, 125, 126, 127
Rapanos v. United States, 9–10, 125–44; background information, 128–30; decision, 143–44; dissent, 143–44; petition granted, 129–30
Regents of the University of California v. Alan Bakke, 36, 98, 100, 105
Rehnquist, William H. (chief justice), 27; on abortion, 47–48; on audio of oral arguments, 3; on *Bush v. Gore,* 66–67; on *Chandler v. Miller,* 113, 118–19, 124; on diversity, 105; on *Glickman v. Wileman Brothers and Elliott Inc.,* 83–84; opinion on the Clean Water Act, 128–29; on oral arguments, 5, 6, 7, 93–94; on parade statute and fees, 34–36; on *Rapanos v. United States,* 128; on religion in the public school system, 18; on the Tenth Amendment, 123
religion, 8, 11, 24; Jehovah's Witness, 27. See also *Elk Grove Unified School District v. Newdow*
Roberts, John G., Jr. (chief justice), viii, 10, 99; on audio of oral arguments, 3; nomination of, 129; on *Randall v. Sorrell,* 148, 151–52, 156; on *Rapanos v. United States,* 134–35, 139, 142
Roe v. Wade, 8, 26, 34, 43, 44, 48, 53, 58; retention of ruling, 59–60
Rule of Five, 21
Rumsfeld v. Padilla, 3
Russert, Tim, 40

Scalia, Antonin G. (justice), 9; on abortion, 49–51; on affirmative action, 108; on *Bush v. Gore,* 66–67, 69; on *Chandler v. Miller,* 113, 115–16, 118, 124; on diversity, 106–7; on *Glickman v.*

Scalia, Antonin G. (*continued*)
Wileman Brothers and Elliott Inc., 82–83, 87, 88; grant of stay in *Bush v. Gore*, 63; on *Grutter v. Bollinger*, 102–3; motion to seek recusal of, 13–14; opinion on *Forsyth County, Georgia v. the Nationalist Movement*, 37; opinion on *Rapanos v. United States*, 143; on oral arguments, 5; on parade statute and fees, 27; on police protection, 30–31; on *Randall v. Sorrell*, 149, 150, 154; on *Rapanos v. United States*, 128, 131, 134, 139–40; silence of, 30; on spousal-notice provision for abortion, 57; on television coverage, 40–41; on Title VII, 160–61, 164, 167–68
Second Circuit Court of Appeals, 145
Senate Judiciary Committee, 46, 47
sexual discrimination, 158. See also *United Automobile, Aerospace, and Agricultural Implement Workers of America (UAAAIWA) v. Johnson Controls Inc.*; women
Silberman, Lawrence (judge), 130
Sixth Circuit Court of Appeals, 127–28
Skinner, Secretary of Transportation et al. v. Railway Labor Executives' Association et al., 111n1
Slate.com, 4
Socratic method, 7
Solid Waste Agency of Northern Cook County (SWANCC) v. U.S. Army Corps of Engineers, 128, 135, 141
Sorrell, William H., 145–57
Souter, David H. (justice): on abortion, 46–47; on *Bush v. Gore*, 68–69; on cameras in the courtroom, 70–71; on *Chandler v. Miller*, 118, 122; as dissenter in *Bush v. Gore*, 67; on *Glickman v. Wileman Brothers and Elliott Inc.*, 81–82, 88; on *Grutter v. Bollinger*, 102; on parade statute and fees, 29–30; on *Randall v. Sorrell*, 155; on *Rapanos v. United States*, 132–34; on spousal-notice provision for abortion, 56, 57; on television coverage, 40; on the Tenth Amendment, 123
speech, 20. See also *Forsyth County, Georgia v. the Nationalist Movement*
Starr, Kenneth W., 57–58
Stevens, John Paul (justice): on abortion, 47; on affirmative action, 108; on *Chandler v. Miller*, 122; on *Glickman v. Wileman Brothers and Elliott Inc.*, 85, 87; on *Grutter v. Bollinger*, 101–2; listening to oral arguments, 21; opinion on *Glickman v. Wileman Brothers and Elliott Inc.*, 95; on *Rapanos v. United States*, 137–38; on religion in the public schools, 18; on spousal-notice provision for abortion, 55, 57–58
Stoepker, Timothy A., 137–38
Storer, Norman, Meyer v. Grant, 120
Strossen, Nadine, 43
Stubbs, Robert, 27, 28
Suter, William, 26, 78
SWANCC. See *Solid Waste Agency of Northern Cook County (SWANCC) v. U.S. Army Corps of Engineers*

television, U.S. Supreme Court and, 39–41
Tenth Amendment, 28, 123
Terminiello v. Chicago, 32
Texaco v. Pennzoil, 70
Thomas, Clarence (justice), 25, 26; on abortion, 46–47; on *Bush v. Gore*, 66–67; as junior justice, 35–37; opposition to, 47; on oral arguments, 93; on politics, 69; on *Rapanos v. United States*, 128
Thornburgh, Richard, 111
Time Inc. v. Hill, 10, 169–78
Title VII, 158, 159, 167. See also *United Automobile, Aerospace, and Agricultural Implement Workers of America (UAAAIWA) v. Johnson Controls Inc.*
Tribe, Laurence, 70
Trop v. Dulles, 21n1

UAAAIWA. See *United Automobile, Aerospace, and Agricultural Implement Workers of America (UAAAIWA) v. Johnson Controls Inc.*
UAW. *See* United Automobile Workers

United Automobile, Aerospace, and Agricultural Implement Workers of America (UAAAIWA) v. Johnson Controls Inc., 10, 158–68
United Automobile Workers (UAW), 158
United States v. Riverside Bayview Homes, 132, 138
United States v. United Foods, Inc., 96
University of Michigan Law School. See *Grutter v. Bollinger*
U.S. Army Corps of Engineers, 125, 127, 131
U.S. Circuit Court of Appeals for the Third Circuit, 45–46
U.S. Congress: 1954 Act, 11; Agricultural Marketing Agreement Act, 74, 81
U.S. Constitution, 11; as jurisdiction of the Supreme Court, 21; privacy and, 34. *See also* individual amendments
U.S. Court of Appeals for the Eleventh Circuit, 23
U.S. Court of Appeals for the Ninth Circuit, 76
U.S. District Court for the Eastern District of Wisconsin, 159
U.S. District Court for the Northern District of Georgia, 23
U.S. Environmental Protection Agency, 125, 127
U.S. Supreme Court: audio transcript, 2–3; "Bible," 22; guidelines for appearance before, 8n4; overview, 1–3; personalization of court cases, 14–15; politics and, 44–45; process of, 3–4; public and, 2; Rule of Five, 21; television coverage of, 39–40; "Ten Commandments of Oral Advocacy," 8, 11–19; written arguments, 2
U.S. v. Frame, 80, 80n6

Vermont. See *Randall v. Sorrell*

Warren, Earl (chief justice), 10, 170
Warren Court, 21–22
Washington Post, 39
water rights, federal power and, 126–28
Wattleton, Faye, 44, 45–46
Webster, Daniel, vii
Webster v. Reproductive Health Services, 46
wetlands, pollutants and, 127. See *Rapanos v. United States;* water rights
White, Byron R. (justice): opinion on *Forsyth County, Georgia v. the Nationalist Movement*, 37; on oral arguments, 6; on spousal-notice provision for abortion, 57; on *Time Inc. v. Hill*, 172, 175, 176; on Title VII, 167
white supremacy, 8
Williams, Hosea, 22, 23
Winter, Ralph K. (judge), 153
women: discrimination against, 159; equality of, 49–50; rights movement in America, 43, 48, 158–59; working under hazardous conditions while pregnant, 10. *See also* abortion; *Planned Parenthood of Southeastern Pennsylvania v. Casey;* pregnancy; sexual discrimination; *United Automobile, Aerospace, and Agricultural Implement Workers of America (UAAAIWA) v. Johnson Controls Inc.*
Wright, Brenda, 155–56

Text design by Paula Newcomb

Typesetting by Delmastype, Ann Arbor, Michigan

Text font: Sabon

Jan Tschichold designed Sabon in 1964 for the three metal type technologies of the time: foundry type for hand composition, linecasting, and single-type machine composition. Tschichold loosely based his design on types from the 1592 specimen sheet issued by the Egenolff-Berner foundry: a 14-point roman attributed to Claude Garamond, and an italic attributed to Robert Granjon. Sabon was the typeface name chosen for this twentieth century revival and joint venture in production; this name avoided confusion with other fonts connected with the names of Garamond and Granjon.

Classic, elegant, and extremely legible, Sabon is one of the most beautiful Garamond variations.

—*courtesy* linotype.com